CDL STUDY GUIDE 2024-2025

BONUS
SCAN THE QR CODE INSIDE AND GET 200 PRINTABLE FLASHCARDS

DETAILED ANSWER EXPLANATIONS

SUITABLE FOR ALL CLASSES AND ENDORSEMENTS

STRAIGHT-TO-THE-POINT REVIEW CHAPTERS WITH COMPREHENSION CHECK QUESTIONS

8 FULL-LENGTH PRACTICE TESTS

THE ALL-IN-ONE TOOL YOU NEED TO GET YOUR LICENSE ON YOUR FIRST TRY

Bonus Flashcards

Dear student, thank you for the trust you are giving us by choosing our "CDL Study Guide 2024". Go to page 86 to receive your 200 printable bonus Flashcards now.

Table of Contents

Introduction

Most people skip this part of the book and go directly to chapter one, so congratulations on being thorough and orderly. You're already off to a good start. I'll spare you the prattle about how repercussions of the pandemic have created a desperate need for certified drivers and how you can make great money doing it and how the open road is the American dream and other inspirational poetic dribble other study guides start out with. But instead, I am going to tell you why I wrote this book and why everything you're about to read is verified reliable information.

I don't really want to pay six bucks for a single chicken nugget.

The fewer truck drivers there are the more shortages there are going to be and the higher the prices are going to go thanks to our capitalist overlords. It is in everyone's best interests, especially mine, that you pass this test with flying colors and get go on the road as quickly as possible so the economists can't justify making things worse than they already are.

There is a lot to know when it comes to commercial driving, and somewhat limited space in this book, and even more limited time for you to learn it. To keep our cost of printing down and not overwhelm you, we're going to be paraphrasing most of the general information you'll find in your state CDL Handbook.

Now, wait! Before you start getting upset thinking you just wasted your money, have you actually looked at your state CDL handbook yet? Otherwise, I suggest you download a copy from your state DMV website (don't worry, it's free,) and scroll through it a little. Depending on what state you're in, you're looking at anywhere from 150-250 pages of almost solid text. are you sure you want to read through all that while trying to pick out the specs of information you actually need to know?

If you do, I'm curious about what set of circumstances led you to pursue this career and not something more akin to a stenographer. But for us average humans and truck driving dogs, this guide should be a much more appealing and helpful read.

What This Guide Is

This guide is written to get you familiar with the rules and concepts you'll need for the Commercial Driver's License test in plain understandable English. It has been written to encourage information retention, and give the best possible advantage to readers starting with zero knowledge of commercial driving.

What This Guide Isn't

This guide is not a list of copy and pasted information you could easily find for yourself for free online. It is also not page after page of practice tests you can also find for free, or some scam "guaranteed" to make you pass your test the first time.

The only thing that can make you pass your test is you, though I'll do my damndest to help for the sake of my chicken nuggets.

How to Get the Most Out of This Study Guide

How you use this book is up to you, but it was designed with a certain methodology in mind. The chapters have been broken up to be short enough to read in one sitting, and I would advise you to read through the entire thing from start to finish at least once even if you're not taking all the endorsement tests. Which you probably shouldn't try to do anyway.

Even if you're not taking the test for, say, air brakes, it's still a good idea to know how they work and what their limitations are when you encounter another vehicle that does have them on the road.

I've even covered some additional points that may be that may be of use outside the test, along with some of the more interesting factoids I've picked up during my career, like how you can legally bring up to 100 lbs of uranium onto a city bus according to federal law.

Getting Ready to Get Started

Before we can start going over what you'll need to know, we should probably go over where you'll need to go and what you'll need to get the process started, especially since this process has changed dramatically since several new federal regulations went into effect in February of 2022. And when I say a lot, I mean a *lot* has changed. The first big change being the introduction of a little nightmare called the ELDT.

Step One: Finding an ELDT-Certified School

It used to be that the first step toward getting your Commercial Driver's License was the same one as getting your regular driver's license: do the written test and get your permit. Alas, no more. Now your first step is to sign up at an accredited CDL school and complete the Entry Level Driver Training (ELDT).

But wait, I lied. That's not actually the first step. The real first step is finding a CDL school that's actually ELDT accredited, which is not all of them. In fact, as of November of 2022—ten months after the new federal laws went into effect—not even *most* CDL schools are ELDT accredited.

Why? Well, there's a very complex answer to that question that has to do with a lot of algorithms and statistics, but the simple answer is money. Any CDL school that isn't ELDT accredited is now a legal scam. How do you avoid getting scammed? Go to the FMCSA Training Provider Registry at https://tpr.fmcsa.dot.gov/ type your address into the location finder, and click that little magnifying glass to pull up a list of accredited in-person, online, and travel providers that will actually be worth your time and money. And I hope you have an ample supply of both because it'll take you between 3–20 days to complete the course depending on your provider, and you'll have to fork over anywhere between $2,500 to upwards of $8,500 just to have the privilege of getting to take the written test after you get that federally certified piece of paper.

Now, I'm sure some of you looked at those numbers, felt a surge of panic and immediately jumped on Google to check if I was pulling your leg. If you have, I'm sure you're looking at advertisements saying that you can get your ELDT for as little as $25–$75. But before you click that link and think all your problems are going to be solved, remember what I said before. Any CDL school that's not ELDT certified is a legal scam. If you don't find it through the office Training Provider Registry I showed you above, it's worthless to you. To put it in trucker terminology, it's registry or bust.

Step Two: Getting Your ELDT Certification

Now that you've found a properly accredited CDL training center that works for you, you have the proper time set aside for classes, and the necessary funds to pay your tuition, I suggest you do two things immediately. First, go buy a lottery ticket because the stars are clearly aligned in your favor, and second, relax. The one good thing I can say about this EDLT mess is that it makes a good driving school a requirement, which means your going to get the one thing I can't give you: hands-on, practical training.

There are 31 federally mandated theoretical assessments, as well as 19 federally mandated training courses that you're going to have to complete to get your ELDT certificate. Now again, relax. We're going to go over everything you need to complete those 31 theoretical assessments—which is just a fancy way of saying test questions—in the next several chapters of this book, and the behind-the-wheel courses are going to be conducted in the safest most controlled conditions you could ask for. Plus, it's pretty simple stuff. The federal government came up with this, do you really think it's going to be difficult?

One last thing, I'm sure you've been asking why you have to take the ELDT when you already have to take the written and driving exams too. The honest answer is this was decided by the federal government; it doesn't have to make sense.

The official answer is a bit convoluted, but the best way to explain it is to think of the ELDT as your personal steering wheel, and the other tests as the actual vehicles you're going to be driving. You need the steering wheel to drive anything, but it's useless on its own. There are several different CDL licenses that all require specific training to operate. Fortunately, we'll be going over all that specific training in the appropriate chapters later on.

Sign Up for Your Written Test

Alright, good job getting that ELDT—see, I told you it wasn't difficult. Now it's on to the written test. Finding a free slot is not particularly difficult, even in a busy city, but it's always best to check. Before you actually head down to your closest DMV outlet make sure to call ahead and confirm that they offer all the tests for the endorsements you're after. Some DMV outlets might not be qualified to give you a test for a hazmat endorsement, or anything other than a bus endorsement. It's weird, and kind of rare, but it does happen so just double check.

As you talk to them, ask how much the test is going to be and what kind of payments they accept. Some places still don't take anything but debit or cash. The price you can expect to pay pretty much anywhere ranges from $35–$70 depending upon your state, unless you're in Alaska where you're looking at $120 per try.

But wait, we're still not done with the ELDT nonsense! Before you can be permitted to sign up the DMV outlet will need to verify through the State Drivers Licence Agency that your ELDT is certified as complete through the Department of Transportation, which has to get the verification from the accredited CDL school you found through the FMCSA Training Provider Registry. Now, how long is that going to take? Well, when you graduate your CDL school should give you a rough estimate of when you can take the written test along with your diploma.

Though let's be real, the state government, the federal government, and a civilian company all have to agree that you did what you did. You're looking at anywhere from 7 hours to 2 weeks depending on the holidays and the position of the moon.

Once that's all finally taken care of, you will finally have the option to schedule your test. A word of warning, however, you're only allowed only a certain number of failures for each section of the test. This means that even if you pass all the written tests, if you forget to fasten your seatbelt before starting the engine three times in a row, you'll need to wait 3 to 6 months depending on what state you're in, pay another entrance fee, and start the process from the beginning! Fortunately, the one thing you don't have to get again is the ELDT.

Oh, one last thing. You're going to need to bring a couple forms of ID with you when you go to take your test. The person you called on the phone earlier should have told you exactly what to bring already, but the standard driver's license, social security card and birth certificate combo should work.

Getting in Driving Time

Congratulations! You've passed the written tests and received your shiny new Commercial Learner's Permit (CLP). Now all you need is the hours, right? Wrong! You've already gotten those thanks to that CDL school you had to sign up for to get your ELDT. Yes, you got your hours in *before* you got your learner's permit. No, it doesn't make any sense, just be glad you're done.

However, just because you've gotten your hours in doesn't mean you can just sit and twiddle your thumbs while you wait for your driving test to be scheduled. You actually now have everything you need to get your first commercial driving job!

Employers need drivers, so you can get free, or even paid hours behind the wheel with an experienced driver training you on real-world jobs. Plus, you'll already have a job ready and waiting for you when you pass! It's a win-win!

If you decide to choose this route, there are a few considerations to keep in mind.

- It's still a job application, so you'll need a resume and probably want to get a haircut for the interview.
- Do *not* apply until you have your CLP in your hands.

Employers want someone who can start immediately, they aren't going to waste time on someone who, in their eyes at least, might not even pass the test.

Sign Up for Your Driving Test

This should be fairly easy depending on where you did your written test. After you get your CLP, ask at the front desk where the closest practical exam is held. They should already have directions ready for you.

Sign up for the driving test as soon as possible. Most states require you to wait 14 days minimum between passing your written test and taking your driving test, but space is limited so signing up for your test as soon as you have secured access to a practice vehicle is vital. It's not that uncommon to have to wait over a month for a slot to become available, so don't sleep on it!

Another piece of advice I want to give you is to make sure you get what's called a "Real ID" version of your CDL once you pass your driving test. If you've been to an airport in the last 5 years you've probably heard of Real IDs at least in passing.

They're essentially state-issued IDs with more advanced security features built into them.

While not all commercial driving jobs require you to have a Real ID it is quickly becoming the standard, especially if the job requires you to cross state lines. Just fork out the extra $10 for the Real ID version of your CDL now so you will not have to buy a new license later.

Medical Certificate Requirements

The FMCSA has come up with some extremely confusing and convoluted rules about who can and can not operate commercial vehicles. These rules were made even more confusing when they got to the state level. Fortunately, you don't need to know them. Unfortunately, you will need to get a Medical Examiner's Certificate (MEC).

Getting a MEC is a pain in every sense. It requires you to go to a federally certified medical examiner and pay anywhere from $50–$100 depending on your state to have them check you over and determine if you're healthy enough to drive something that could plow through a shopping center.

But before you start groaning at having to pay yet another exorbitant federal fee, I have good news for you. Since a MEC is required by federal law, most employers will cover the cost for you! If you were able to land that on-the-job training I mentioned before, ask your employer about scheduling your medical examination if they haven't brought it up to you already.

You'll want to get this taken care of soon, because if you have any preexisting conditions like diabetes, you wear glasses, or your state is just really vindictive, there is a chance that you'll have to send your MEC via mail or fax (or email if you are *very* lucky), to your local Drivers License Division before you are allowed to take your driving test.

Yes, your DLD, *not* your DMV, it's a separate place entirely.

How the Written Test Works

In a simple world, I could just give you the 50 questions that will be on the general knowledge test along with the 30 you'll get for each endorsement test, but the DMV is government-funded, so nothing can ever be simple. There is a large pool of 200 questions for the general knowledge test, and more pools of 100 questions for each of the endorsement tests.

But there's also good news, and that's that you don't have to answer all the questions in order to pass. Just like the standard driver's license test, you will be taking the CDL on a computer and as soon as you answer either 80% of the questions correctly or 20% of the questions incorrectly the test will end. That means you need to get 40 questions correct on the general knowledge test, and 18–24 questions correct on each of the endorsements to pass.

The trick is that there's a skip button at the bottom of the screen that will let you pass on a question without answering at no penalty. The question goes to the back of the 50 question queue, meaning you can answer all the questions you're confident on before you have to start guessing.

Basically, if you don't know the answer, press the skip button. It'll save you a lot of retests.

Chapter Questions

1. How many questions are there in the CDL general knowledge test?

a) 100
b) 50
c) 25
d) 30

2. What is a realistic amount you can expect to pay (on average) for your written test?

a) $5-$10
b) $25-$50
c) $30-$70
d) $120

3. Why should you get a Real ID version of your CDL?

a) It looks cooler
b) Many driving jobs require a Real ID
c) It's safer
d) It's mandatory

4. What does MEC stand for?

a) Medical Exemption Certificate
b) Medical Examiner's Certificate
c) Mariner's Examiner's Certificate
d) Medical Executive Certificate

5. Do you like this book?

a) Definitely
b) Absolutely
c) 100%
d) All of the above

Chapter Answers

1. b)
2. c)
3. c)
4. b)
5. b)

General Information Part 1: Safe Driving

Alright, now that we've got a plan in place let's start going over what you'll need to know to pass the test.

Basic Controls

Assuming that you're familiar with driving a non-commercial sized vehicle, and you better be, controlling a commercial-sized vehicle should be a pretty easy transition, except for the fact that everything is way harder and much more dangerous.

Here are some basic tips and things you'll need to know for the test:

- Fasten your seatbelt before you start the engine.
- Accelerate slowly and carefully.
- Hold the steering wheel firmly on a horizontal line across the center of the wheel. Think nine and three, not ten and two.
- Turn slowly and carefully, this vehicle is much bigger than what you're probably used to.
- Come to a stop smoothly and evenly. Hard braking = disaster
- Back up like a puppy might dive under your tires at any moment.
- If your vehicle has a manual transmission, know that you have horribly wronged someone in a previous life and this is your penance.
- When turning, use your turn signal well in advance and keep it on all the way through the turn.

Manual Transmissions

Manual transmissions are a dying breed, but they're unfortunately still prevalent enough that the CDL test continues to include questions about them. This is because while most of the moderate to large companies you'll drive for have updated to automatic transmissions, many smaller local companies still use older models with the dreaded manual transmission.

While you will have the option to test with either an automatic or a manual transmission vehicle in the driving portion, you don't get a choice on questions pertaining to them showing up on your general knowledge exam.

Shifting Gears

If there's anything many of the newbies hate, it's trying to shift gears in one. It seems to them like a macabre dance of esoteric intent, designed only to intimidate new drivers and please the demon that lives inside all manual transmission engines so it does not burn out the clutch and render the vehicle inoperable.

But you need to know how to do it for the test, so here are the basic steps to shifting up using the double shift method outlined in your CDL handbook:

- Releasing the accelerator, press the clutch, and shift to neutral all at the same time.
- Now release the clutch.

- Let the engine and gear speed slow down to the revolutions per minute (RPM) required for the next gear (more on that later).
- Once you're at the proper RPM, push in the clutch and shift to the desired higher gear simultaneously.
- Now release the clutch and press the accelerator at the same time.

This instead is the procedure for the downshifting:

- Release the throttle, push the clutch while shifting into neutral at the same time.
- At this point, release the clutch.
- Push on the accelerator and raise the engine and transmission gear speed to the required RPM to the lower gear.
- Press the clutch and, simultaneously, shift to the lower gear.
- Now release the clutch and push on the accelerator at the same time.

The best way I've found to remember it is to go back to the dance analogy.

- Two-step to neutral
- Unclutch
- Adjust
- Clutch Shift
- Two-step again.

Feel free to figure out your own method.

How to tell if you need to shift gears

I'm sure you're curious as to how you know what gear goes to what speed. There are two methods outlined in the CDL handbook that you'll need to know for the test.

The first is referred to as the Engine Speed method. Next to the speedometer is a smaller dial or digital read-out called a tachometer. The tachometer measures engine rotation, and whenever it hits the top you'll know it's time to shift up.

The second method is called the Road Speed method. All it is is knowing what gear you need to be in based on how fast you're going and raw experience. However, which gear is best for which speed changes from vehicle to vehicle.

The Engine Speed method isn't always accurate either, especially for older trucks that have had a lot of work done on them, but these are the two methods you'll need to know for the test.

Visibility and Blind Spots

While blind spots are specific to what kind of vehicle you're driving, there are a few trouble spots all commercial vehicles share.

Following, the visibility and blind spot information you need for the test:

- You should always be looking 12-15 seconds ahead, or two of your own vehicle's lengths, whichever is furthest.
- According to CDL handbooks, the average driver has a reaction time of 3/4ths of a second.
- A green light is considered "stale" if it has been green longer than 20 seconds.
- You should treat any stale green light like a yellow light.
- You can not see directly behind you while driving most commercial vehicles, this makes backing up extremely dangerous.
- Check and double-check your mirrors on both sides when:
- Making a turn
- Signaling a lane change
- Making a lane change
- Upon completing a lane change
- Regularly to check for tire fires, lose cargo, and undead highwaymen coming to claim their toll

Make Yourself Known

While it is vital for you to know where other vehicles and pedestrians are, it also helps to make sure other drivers are aware of you too. While you may think a commercial vehicle would be easy to spot, nearly 300 fatalities per year occur because people weren't paying attention and somehow missed the 800 tons of metal and diesel they ran into!

You have three main tools to keep people alert to your presence: the horn, the signal lights, and emergency warning devices such as reflective triangles and road flares.

Here's what you need to keep in mind for each:

The Horn

- Tap lightly in urban areas.
- Exercise caution when using your horn to alert drivers near you to your presence as it can startle them and cause them to make erratic movements.
- With that said, don't be afraid to use it when you need to get someone's attention.

Signal Lights

- Use your lights to signal both before and during a turn.
- Flash your low beams during the day to get the attention of drivers and pedestrians in place of your horn. Do not use high beams because they can blind drivers and cause them to move erratically.
- Turn on low beams during the day when there is limited visibility, such as in fog, rain or darkness to make yourself more visible to oncoming vehicles.
- Engage your vehicle's four-way emergency flashers when you pull off to the side of the road, especially in limited visibility as tail lights will not communicate that your vehicle is stationary to other drivers.

Emergency Warning Devices

- If you stop on or near a one-way or divided highway, set warning devices 10 feet, 100 feet and 200 feet towards oncoming traffic to warn them of your stopped vehicle
- If you stop on a two-lane road or undivided highway carrying traffic in both directions place your warning devices 10 feet and 100 feet away from the front and back of the vehicle.
- If the view of your vehicle could be obstructed by a hill, turn or anything else within 500 feet, make sure your warning devices are visible from the other side of the obstruction.

Remember, 10, 100, and 200 feet behind you if traffic is one way. 10 and 100 feet in front and behind if traffic goes both ways, and if there's any kind of obstruction within 500 feet of your vehicle make sure your warnings are visible from the other side.

Stopping Distance

If you are traveling at 30 miles an hour, on a perfectly level and dry road with completely clear visibility it will take you over 153 feet to come to a full stop. We are talking about a length close to half football field to stop in perfect conditions on a typical urban street.

Add a little bit of rain to that equation and the distance increases to nearly 200 feet!

Every time you double your speed your total stopping distance increases by a factor of four. It doesn't double or triple, it *quadruples*!

The calculation outlined in your CDL handbook is:

Perception Distance + Reaction Distance + Breaking Distance = Total Stopping Distance

You will need to memorize this exact formula. While you will probably never use it in real life, it is one of the most common questions on the test and one of the most commonly missed. It's almost always phrased confusingly or given with very similar looking answers, so you can expect to see a question that looks like this:

1. **Total stopping distance equals**

a) Perception distance + reaction distance + braking distance.
b) reaction distance + braking distance.
c) reaction distance + viewing distance + braking distance.
d) Braking distance + stopping.

The best way I know to remember this is Perception Reaction Breaking or P.R.B.

Here are some additional facts you'll need to know.

- While the average driver reaction time is 3/4ths of a second, the average *perception* time for an alert driver is 1 and 3/4ths of a second.
- Your braking distance is dependent on a lot of factors including your speed, the total weight of the vehicle, what kind of breaks you're using, and how well maintained they are.
- For the purposes of the test, just say your stopping distance is one American football field.

Leaving the Vehicle

Most people aren't going to want to mess with your vehicle once you park it, but there's always a possibility that someone will, and always a guarantee that gravity is going to ruin your day whenever you give it half a chance.

To prevent this, always do the same routine before you leave your vehicle.

- Set the parking brakes or chock the wheels
- Take the keys with you
- Shock the wheels if you are on any level of incline or decline

The second step should be a no-brainer, (though you would be shocked at how many drivers leave the keys inside the cabin,) the last step is often overlooked. It takes an extra minute to chock your wheels, but it is important to do if you are parking on anything but a perfectly level surface.

It's also a common question on the test, so make sure you put it to memory.

Chapter Questions

1. You should put on your seat belt:

a) Before you start the engine
b) After you check your mirrors
c) From outside the vehicle
d) Only when you' re instructed to do so

2. Shifting Gears is like:

a) A fine wine
b) Making a souffle
c) A dance
d) A puzzle

3. You should slow down _____ entering fog.

a) After
b) Before
c) While
d) Silent Hill

4. Use your turn signal

a) Before changing lanes and all the way through
b) Before changing lanes, but turn it off when you start
c) Never
d) Only when actually turning

5. A driver has an average reaction time of

a) 0.5 seconds
b) 3/4ths of a second
c) 4 seconds
d) 1 second

6. A stale light:

a) Is a light that's been green for 20 or more seconds
b) Should be treated like a yellow light
c) Is crunchy
d) Both A and B

7. When leaving the vehicle:

a) Activate the parking brake and take out the keys
b) Leave the keys in the cabin
c) Always dive out John Wick style
d) Set the Emergency Brake

8. Manual Transmissions:

a) Are delightful
b) Are a dying breed
c) Are easy to use
d) Are safer and more reliable

9. In urban areas:

a) Tap your horn
b) Blare your horn
c) Never use your horn
d) Use it to signal a turn

10. You should always:

a) Accelerate carefully and keep your hands at 9 and 3
b) Accelerate carefully and keep your hands at 10 and 2
c) Floor it and keep your hands out the window
d) Accelerate as needed and keep your hands on the wheel

11. How far should you look ahead to drive safely?

a) 12-15 seconds ahead, or two of your own vehicle's lengths, whichever is furthest.
b) No more than 5 feet ahead
c) Up to the vehicle in front of you
d) There is no safety distance commonly recognized as valid

Chapter Answers

1. a)
2. c)
3. b)
4. a)
5. b)
6. d)
7. a)
8. b)
9. a)
10. a)
11. a)

General Information Part 2: Weather

Unless you eat a bowl full of four-leaf clovers and rabbit's feet every morning, you're not going to spend all your time driving in optimal conditions.

Night

Visibility is greatly reduced, you're probably tired, and the U.S. government has officially recognized the existence of U.F.O.s.

On the plus side, the roads are emptier, and the best radio talk shows are always on late at night.

Here's what you have to know about night driving for the test:

- If you feel sleepy, do not drive. Stop at the nearest safe place and sleep.
- Caffeine is no substitute for sleep and the resulting caffeine crash can lead to a *fatal* crash.
- Do not were sunglasses at night. You do not look cool. You just look like a crash waiting to happen.
- Perform a complete vehicle inspection prior to sundown and ensure that all lights and reflectors are functional and clean.
- Use high beams when safe and legal to do so.
- Avoid blinding others. Turn off high beams within 500 feet of an oncoming vehicle or when following one.
- Avoid glare from the oncoming vehicles by looking slightly to the right of the right lane or edge marking.
- Keep interior lights off and ensure that instrument lights are as low as possible while still being visible. This is to keep your eyes adjusted to the outside light levels.
- Turn on your headlights at least half an hour before sunset.

Fog

When driving in fog your vision is severely impaired. This should not be news to you.

Here's what the CDL handbook says to do when driving in fog:

- Slow down *before* you enter the fog.
- In addition, use low-beam and fog lights for the very best visibility, even at night. High beams will actually obscure your vision in fog
- Be on alert for other drivers who have not turned on their own lights.
- Turn on your 4-way emergency flashers so approaching vehicles will have the best chance possible to see you.
- Listen for traffic you cannot see. (This is listed in the handbook as an official step and may appear on the test, but it's realistically very stupid advice since you're inside a sound-resistant cabin behind a loud engine.)
- Do not attempt to pass other vehicles.
- Avoid stopping along the roadside unless absolutely necessary.

Winter Driving

Reduce your speed by a third if you encounter any of the following on the road during cold weather:

- Shaded Areas
- Bridges
- Outside temperatures at or greater than 30 degrees Fahrenheit
- Any roads that look wet
- Any roads that are not properly illuminated
- Your windshield or mirrors begin icing over (If a moving vehicle is getting icy you can bet your butt the ground is too!)

The most dangerous hazard you'll encounter in cold weather is black ice. You're probably already aware of what black ice is, but for the purposes of the test keep these things in mind:

- Black ice isn't actually black. It's a thin layer of ice clear enough that you can see the road underneath it, rendering the ice nearly invisible no matter what the road color.
- On snow and ice, even for simple common sense, you should reduce your speed by at least half.

Wait, didn't we say earlier to reduce your speed by a third if you see any signs of slippery roads? Yes, but that's for *possible* slippery roads. If you know there's ice ahead, drop down to at least half of the total speed limit.

Doesn't this make the test annoyingly confusing? Yes. Yes, it does.

Wet Roads

Wet roads can be equally dangerous as icy roads, especially during the beginning of a storm. Vehicle pollution collects on road surfaces, and when things get wet that pollution turns into an oil slick. The more time it has been since the last rain, the more slippery the road will be.

The oil usually washes away completely after about an hour of solid rain, but after that, you need to be aware of possible flooding and water pooling on the road. Never try to challenge mother nature when it comes to flooding. I don't care how big and tricked out your rig is, the flood is always going to win.

If you see water rushing over the road, find a dryer detour or wait it out, even if it doesn't look like much. Running or pooled water can hide a plethora of dangers; unexpected potholes, sharp debris, evil clowns washed up from the sewers, anything!

Even if the water isn't hiding anything malicious, heavy rain and deep water can make your breaks wet. Wet breaks are very dangerous since they impair your ability to stop evenly. The fact that one side of your vehicle is slowing down faster than

the other can result in the vehicle pulling to one side. This is especially dangerous if you're pulling a trailer since it could cause it to jackknife and rollover. Now how are you going to escape from the clown?

Hydroplaning and Skids

Hydroplaning is where some form of liquid, usually water as the name implies, causes a vehicle's tires to lose traction with the ground and begin to skid. The vehicle will have little to no response to steering or breaking, which can be a big problem if there's something ahead of you like another vehicle, a puppy orphanage, or a cliff.

If you begin to hydroplane do not try to steer harder. Instantly remove your foot from the accelerator and push the clutch (even an automatic vehicle has a clutch.) This will enable the wheels to turn without restraint and find their grip again. Let the vehicle slow on its own and turn gently if needed. Again, do NOT try to make a hard turn. The wheels will lose traction again and you'll be completely out of control. Regaining control using this method can take a few seconds, so if you're hydroplaning or skidding directly in front of that cliff, well… let's just hope enough of you is recognizable to collect insurance.

The best ways to protect against hydroplaning are to reduce speed on wet roads and properly maintain your tires. Minimum tread depth is 4/32-inch for the front wheels and 2/32-inch for all other tires. The phenomenon of hydroplaning can occur as low as 30 mph, and skids can happen at any speed on ice and slick roads.

Play it safe and respect mother nature. Even the world's biggest eighteen-wheeler is nothing more than a Hot Wheels car to her.

Extreme Heat

On the other end of the thermometer, here is what you need to keep in mind when driving in temperatures above 90 degrees Fahrenheit.

- Pay special attention to tire pressure when driving in extreme heat. Hot air expands, so a blow out or a tire fire becomes more likely the hotter it gets.
- Do not let the air out of tires that are overinflated due to extreme heat. When the tires cool down again the pressure will be too low and the resulting friction can cause a tire fire. Which is somewhat ironic if you think about it.
- Ensure your engine has adequate oil and coolant during checks.
- Never remove a radiator cap or any other part of a pressurized system until the system has cooled. It runs on steam, don't mess with it until it's properly cool unless you want a face-melting sauna.
- Check that your engine belts are tight and do not have any signs of wear or damage.
- Finally, if anything is leaking, like say a damaged hose or ruptured gasket, you want to get that fixed properly as soon as possible. Patch jobs done with duct tape or similar materials will either melt or catch fire in extreme heat.

Bleeding Roads

Remember how vehicle pollution can create oil slicks on the road when it rains? Well, when it gets very hot and dry for a long period of time the tar in the asphalt can bleed to the surface and create an unstable gel that's not only a skid hazard, but also slightly sticky and near-boiling hot.

Horrifying huh?

Go Slow

High speeds mean high heat, and that means your engine is more likely to overheat. Overheating your engine can result in anything from engine failure and permanent damage, to the engine catching on fire and your truck exploding. Play it cool and take it slow.

Chapter Questions

1. If your brakes get wet, what can happen?

a) Wheel lockup
b) Trailer jackknife
c) Lack of braking power
d) All answers are correct

2. If the engine isn't overheated, is it totally safe to take off the radiator cap?

a) Yes, if the radiator is not damaged.
b) Yes, if there is no overflow.
c) No.
d) Yes.

3. Bleeding roads:

a) Occur in extreme heat and are skidding hazards
b) Occur in extreme cold and are skidding hazards
c) Only happen in horror movies
d) Are a sign of a recent car accident

4. If you start to hydroplane you should

a) Hit the gas
b) Hit the brakes
c) Turn the wheel sharply
d) Engage the clutch

5. If you feel tired while driving you should:

a) Get some coffee
b) Get some booze
c) Get some sleep
d) Get some help

6. In case you find ice on the ground you should reduce your speed by

a) 1/2
b) 1/4
c) 1/3
d) 1/32

7. Reduce your speed by a third of you see:

a) A bridge
b) A shaded area
c) Ice form on your windshield
d) All of the above

8. If your tires swell up from heat you should

a) Stop and let them cool
b) Let out some air
c) Change them
d) Watch out for speed bumps

9. In fog you should turn on your:

a) Radio
b) High Beams
c) 4-way Emergency Lights
d) Cellphone

10. Minimum tread depth is:

a) 2/32-inch for the front wheels and 4/32-inch for all other tires
b) 4/32-inch for the front wheels and 2/32-inch for all other tires
c) 2/32-inch for all tires
d) For losers

11. What can you do to prevent the engine from overheating?

a) Go slowly
b) Spray cold water on the engine at each stop
c) Do not drive when the weather is hot
d) None of the above

Chapter Answers

1. d)
2. c)
3. a)
4. d)
5. c)
6. a)
7. d)
8. a)
9. c)
10. b)
11. a)

General Information Part 3: Hazards

Weather and poor lighting conditions aren't the only hazards that you're going to encounter on the road. You'll also have to deal with pedestrians, fires, distracted drivers, road rage, wild animals, and sub-par diners.

You're on your own for those last two, but I can help with the rest.

Fires

Here are the likely causes of fires you will have to know for your test:

- Road accidents with spilled fuel and improperly used road flares.
- Under-inflated tires and dual tires that are touching
- Shorted electrical systems
- Flammable Cargo that is improperly sealed or ventilated
- Drivers smoking while fueling their vehicles.

If your vehicle happens to spontaneously combust in anyway, facilitate the following fastidious firefighting formula fast!

- Remain calm
- Pull off the road but do not pull into a service station. (Your vehicle is on fire, why in the world would you pull up to a gas station!)
- Call 9-1-1. (Personally, I think "get out of the burning vehicle" should go before "call 9-1-1," but I don't make federal regulations, so what do I know.)
- Do not allow the fire to spread while you wait for emergency services to arrive. If the engine is on fire, turn off the engine as soon as you can and do not try to open the hood. Spray the extinguisher through the grill or underneath is possible.
- You are required to have an A:B:C fire extinguisher in your vehicle, which is a multi-use dry chemical extinguisher designed to work on wood, paper, and cloth fires.
- B:C extinguishers are only effective on electrical and burning liquids.
- When using a fire extinguisher, point it at the base of the fire, and sweep back and forth.
- Continue until whatever was burning has cooled as residual heat could cause the fire to reignite.
- If the cargo is on fire, keep the doors shut. Opening the doors will provide the fire with more oxygen, causing it to burn faster and possibly flare directly into your face. This situation, as you can imagine, is even more dangerous if you are transporting hazardous materials.

Alcohol, Drugs, and Other Inhibitors

Don't drink and drive. Seriously, just *don't*.

Here's what you have to know for the test:

- Federal law prohibits all commercial vehicle operators from drinking while on duty or consuming any intoxicating beverage within four hours *prior* to going on duty.

- The only thing that can really make a person sober is time.
- "Implied consent" means that whenever you are operating a CMV on public roads, you consent to be tested for alcohol in your blood at any time.
- It takes the body about four hours to get rid of the alcohol in four drinks.

Prescription Drugs

Here's what you have to know about prescription drugs for the test:

- Do not use any drugs that can mask fatigue.
- Do not drive while taking any drugs that can cause fatigue or impairment.
- If you are prescribed a new drug by a doctor, always ask how it will impact your driving.
- Read all warnings on over-the-counter medication.

Illness

If you become too sick to operate a vehicle safely then don't try to operate the vehicle! In the case of an emergency, stop at the nearest safe place and call 9-1-1. Nobody wants you on the road if you're going to be throwing up and possibly passing out behind the wheel.

Roadway Work Zones

Slow your butt down in a work zone! Remember when we went over all those blind spots? That goes triple for a work zone. The ground is possibly uneven or unstable, there are people walking around everywhere, speeds are greatly reduced, and there is heavy machinery with their own blind spots that probably aren't expecting anything bigger than a pickup truck to be where you are right now.

Pay attention, obey all posted signs and keep half an eye on your speedometer. It's a bit easy to let your speed start to creep up during long sections of construction. Do anything the workers tell you. If they signal you to stop, then stop. If they tell you your vehicle can't come through the work zone and you'll have to take a detour, don't argue with them! Just do what the nice person in the orange vest says and don't risk your job and theirs because the road looks perfectly fine up ahead to you.

It could be being prepped for explosive demolition for all you know.

Railroad Crossings

Commercial vehicles are the proverbial kings of the highway. You're the biggest thing on the interstate. Every pickup truck envies you, and all eco-friendly hybrids live in semi-electric fear of you.

But if commercial vehicles are royalty, then trains are wrathful gods, and the railroad crossings are their most sacred altars. Do not disrespect the train gods, you won't live to regret it.

Below, the most relevant information about the railroad crossings that you will need for the test:

- Never race a train to a crossing. The train cannot stop, and you can get stuck on the tracks.
- Do not expect to hear a train. The laws of physics make trains surprisingly stealthy.
- Be aware that low-slung and single-axle trucks pulling long trailers are more prone to getting stuck on raised crossings.

- If you become stuck on railroad tracks call 9-1-1 immediately
- It takes 14 seconds for a combination vehicle or bus to free a single track and more than 15 seconds to free a double track.

Mountain Driving and Grades

A grade is just an incline or decline in the road. Unless you drive exclusively in North Dakota or Kansas you're likely going to be driving on a lot of grades. Even if you do live in either of those places, you're still going to need to know how to navigate them because it's part of the test, and because anyone who's in North Dakota or Kansas should be solely focused on leaving there as fast as possible.

Brake Fade

While climbing up a steep grade can be difficult since gravity is constantly trying to convince your vehicle to go the other way, going down is even more dangerous. The only thing that's going to keep you from going out of control on a steed downgrade is your breaks, but using them too much causes them to heat up and lose effectiveness. This is called brake fade, and it usually ends in your vehicle either stuck in an escape ramp or flying off the edge of a cliff.

Since neither of those are desirable outcomes, here is how to avoid brake fade.

First, determine your target safe speed using the following:

- Posted speed limit
- Total weight of the vehicle and cargo
- Road conditions
- Length and steepness of the grade itself

That's the test answer anyway. Realistically, just know your vehicle's limitations. Also, it's usually a bad idea to do anything over 40 mph on a decline.

Once you've got your target safe speed, maintain it using this three-step braking method.

- Apply the brakes until you can feel a definite slowdown.
- Hold the brakes at this position until you have decreased by 5 mph then release the brake. For example: If you're driving 40 mph, then slow down to 35 mph.
- Allow your speed to increase back up to the safe speed and repeat from step 1 until you are on level ground.

While this method is the safest way to take downgrades, it is by no means a guarantee. Brakes can fail from unexpected wear, stress on the engine, and any number of other things. Make sure you know where the escape ramps are along your route prior to driving it. There may be signs down the way as well, but it's best to have a plan. Indeed, most employers will require you to have one.

Driving Emergencies

A driving emergency is what you call the two to three seconds before a driving accident. They're the moments that decide if you're going to continue driving or never drive again. According to the state CDL handbooks, there are two classifications of driving emergencies.

- Traffic emergencies are whenever two or more vehicles are about to collide.
- Vehicle emergencies occur when brakes, tires, or other critical parts fail and there is only one vehicle involved.

The Weaving Maneuver

Here are five things you should keep in mind if you are moments away from a head on collision:

- Stopping is often either impossible or inadvisable. Remember, your stopping distance is measured in minutes, not the few seconds you have to work with.
- Keep both hands on the steering wheel. Commercial vehicles are not known for their easy turning.
- Steering around the obstacle is almost always a better option. However, frantic turning can cause top-heavy vehicles to rollover, so be decisive but not spastic.
- Do not use the brake while you are turning. It can easily lock your wheels, causing you to skid and lose what little control you had.
- Do not turn more than necessary to avoid the obstacle. The sharper your turn is the bigger your chance of rolling over. Even clipping an obstacle is better than totaling your vehicle completely.

Once you're clear of the original problem you're not in the clear yet. You still need to countersteer back on course. If you just turn out of the way of one problem, then you'll have a whole new direction and series of problems to deal with. Try to weave around the obstacle rather than veering away.

Weave to the Right

- Drifting vehicles are more likely to try to return to their own lane when they notice you.
- The shoulder is often the safest lane available to you.
- in an absolute worst-case scenario you won't hit anyone else trying to avoid the moron playing chicken with you.

When Forced to Leave the Road

When you are forced to drive off the road there are some official guidelines to keep in mind.

- Avoid breaking until your speed has decreased to around 20 mph to avoid skidding on loose surfaces.
- Keep a couple of wheels on the paved road to help with control if at all possible.
- Stay on the shoulder if you can.

When Returning to the Road

This is a little counterintuitive, but when you are returning to asphalt from a loose surface like dirt or grass you have to turn sharply and move quickly to get onto it. I know, I've told you to do everything slowly and carefully up to this point, but if you try to go from loose soil to solid ground slowly the tires will gain traction at different times and you could lose control.

This is one of the few times you should turn sharply, so it should be easy to remember the procedure.

- Hold the wheel tightly as you turn sharply back onto the road.
- When both front tires are on the pavement immediately begin counter-steering to course-correct onto the road proper.
- This is another weaving maneuver, so it should all be treated as one action.

Quick Stopping Without Anti-Lock Brakes

The anti-lock brake system (ABS) is one of the most revolutionary and lifesaving advancements in engineering since the seat belt. Actually, it may even be better since it works just as safely for female-bodied people as it does for male-bodied ones.

It's a computerized system designed to keep the tires from locking up and losing traction. ABSs are required for almost all commercial vehicles made after 1999, but if your vehicle doesn't have one, or it stops working suddenly, you'll need to master imitating it with the stab braking technique.

Stab Braking

- Apply your brakes all the way but don't stomp down on them.
- Once you feel your wheels start to lock up, release the brakes so they can gain traction again.
- As soon as the wheels catch the road and start rolling again, reapply the brakes.
- Repeat until you come to a full stop. (Hopefully not a sudden one.)

Retarders

A retarder is a device that can help slow your vehicle without the need for brakes. There are four types of retarders:

- Exhaust
- Engine
- Hydraulic
- Electric

All retarders function the same way. They are manually turned on by the driver and apply separate braking power to the drive wheels whenever the accelerator pedal is fully released.

There are two major drawbacks to using retarders, however. The first is that they can reduce the traction of your drive wheels which can increase the chance and severity of a skid, so you should never use retarders in high risk conditions such as storms or cold weather.

The second drawback is that they make a *lot* of noise. I can't tell you why nobody has been able to invent a retarder that doesn't sound like a malfunctioning helicopter being driven by an angry goose, but I can tell you that using retarders in urban areas can result in expensive fines and tickets for the excessive noise.

Other Drivers

This is indisputably the single most common hazard you are going to encounter. Whether it's road rage, exhaustion, or simple distraction, there is nothing more dangerous than another vehicle.
Here's some of the more common dangers according to the CDL handbook:

Road Rage

If you are being tailgated do not speed up. Keep right to allow the tailgater to pass when they get tired of harassing you. Avoid eye contact and do not do anything to incite the driver.
Yes you could easily grind that irritating little sports car into the rail, but it just isn't worth the fines or the damage to your vehicle. Just turn up the radio, let the idiot lose interest in you, and call their license plate number and other details in to the police when you have a chance to do so safely.
If you happen to see the remains of the vehicle involved in a crash further down the road, you are legally obliged to stop a safe distance away from the crash and wait for the authorities to arrive so that you can tell them about your interaction earlier.
Do not speak to the driver, but be sure to give them a little wave as they're loaded onto the stretcher, or into the back of a police car.

Blocked Vision

It's hard enough trying to see out of your vehicle, but remember it's just as hard for people trying to see around it! Check your mirrors and blind spots for folks who aren't checking theirs.
Intersections, alleyways, and other obstructions can be even more dangerous since you may be able to see only part of a vehicle while it's driver can't see you. Always give any vehicle that is backing out of anything ample space, never assume that they see you.

Ice Cream Trucks

Okay so the Ice Cream truck itself isn't really the issue here. They make a lot of noise and are pretty easy to see. The real danger is the children who like to dash out from behind trees, vehicles, and anything else they can hide behind to get to the ice cream truck.

Pedestrians, Bicyclists, and Children

It's honestly best to just assume that anyone you can see is a sleep deprived clutz with two left feet. It doesn't matter if they're on foot, bike, skateboard, little red wagon, or riding in a baby carriage, somebody *is* going to end up taking a dive in front of your vehicle by accident eventually. Be extra cautious whenever you are traveling in a residential or urban area.

Parked Vehicles

Yes, even a parked vehicle can be a deadly hazard, usually because it's parked somewhere it shouldn't be. Don't assume a vehicle is moving just because it's on the road. Make sure you're looking at those 12-15 seconds ahead at all times, and if you seem to be gaining on a vehicle a little too quickly, it might behoove you to slow down or change lanes. Preferably both.

Cellphone Usage

Don't be a distracted driver either! Texting or using your cellphone for anything other than a GPS or music/podcast player is a fast way to lose your CDL license. Your commercial driver's license will be disqualified for 60 days after two or more convictions of any state law regarding or related to texting while in operation of a commercial vehicle. Three offences within a three year window will disqualify you for three years! Severe, but easy to remember.

If that's not enough to get you to put down the phone, perhaps the fines will. Every ticket for texting while driving a commercial vehicle carries a federally mandated $2,750.00 fine in *addition* to whatever the state charges you. Remember that the next time you have a desire to check your Twitter feed behind the wheel.

Hazardous Material Rules for All Commercial Drivers

While the more dangerous Hazardous Materials will require their own certification and endorsement, there are some classifications of HazMat that can be transported without a license. We'll go into more detail in the appropriate chapter, but there are some basics you will need to know for the general knowledge test.

The Reason for HazMat Rules

The focus on all HazMat rules are threefold:

- Contain the product
- Communicate the risk
- Ensure the safety of the driver and equipment

Warning Labels

Every hazardous material you will transport will come with proper warning and rules for how to load, transport, and unload these items. These rules are communicated in detail on the shipping papers and in general with diamond-shaped hazard labels also known as placards.

Shipping Papers

According to federal law, shipping papers identifying HazMat materials must be kept on top of your other shipping papers and with an additional copy in at least one of the following locations:

- On top of your other shipping papers
- In a pouch in the door on the driver's side
- Within clear view and within reach of the driver while driving

Placards

The diamond-shaped HazMat placards are used to warn others of hazardous materials at a glance. Not all hazardous materials require placards, and a quick rule is that if the HazMat doesn't require a placard, then you don't need a HazMat endorsement to transport it.

Here are some specifics about placards you'll need to know for the general knowledge test:

- Every placard must have four identical placards that are readable from all four directions
- Placards must be at least 9.84 inches (250 mm) square turned upright to a point in a diamond shape.
- All placards must include a four-digit code preceded by the letters "NA" or UN". These codes are used by first responders to identify hazardous materials.

Accident Procedures

When all your preventative measures fail and you end up involved in a road accident of some type, commercial drivers have a few additional responsibilities than other motorists. If you are not seriously hurt your priority is to prevent any further damage or injury. To do that, remember P.A.I.N.S.
P.A.I.N.S. stands for Protect, Alert, Injured, Network, Submit and it will help you remember the proper order and steps of the CDL accident procedure.

Protect

Protect the area and oncoming drivers. One accident can easily lead to another. If your vehicle is involved in the accident but can still be operated safely, move it off to the side or the road and engage your four-way emergency flashers. Commercial vehicles can easily block off roads and create pileups, so if you can move it do so.
Once you're out of the way, or if you can't safely move your vehicle, set out the reflective triangles we talked about earlier to warn oncoming traffic.

Alert

Now that you've done what you can to keep things from getting worse, call 9-1-1 or use your CB radio to call for assistance. Other people should have been doing the same already, but even if they say they did make the call anyway. If the person who made the call is in shock, they may have given wrong information that could cost the paramedics and authorities valuable time.

Injured

The area is reasonably secure and help is on the way. If there is already a qualified person at the accident helping the injured stay out of their way unless asked to assist. If there isn't a doctor in the house, follow these basic first aid steps:

- Don't reposition or move a severely injured person unless unless fire or traffic hazards make it necessary.
- Try stopping severe bleeding by applying direct pressure to the wound.
- Keep the injured person warm.

They may not seem like much, but these three steps can make all the difference while you wait for the paramedics to arrive.

Network

Once help arrives, or if by some miracle nobody was severely hurt, it's time to start exchanging information with everyone involved.
Here's a list of what you should be trying to get:

- Name, address, and phone number of drivers involved in the accident
- License plate number and type of vehicles involved in the accident
- Name and address of the owners of the other vehicles (if different from the drivers)
- Extent of damage to other vehicles or property
- Names and addresses of anyone who was injured or involved in the accident
- Name, badge number, and agency of any officers investigating the accident
- Names and addresses of witnesses
- Exact location of the accident
- Direction of travel of the vehicles involved

If any civilians refuse to give you their information, wait for the authorities and get it from them. Emotions are going to be running high, try not to pressure anyone into blowing their top.

Submit

Submit actually has two directions. The first is to remind you to cooperate with any authority figures investigating or giving care on sight, and the second is to remind you to submit your report to dispatch. Contact your dispatch as soon as it is safe for you to do so and give them all the information you were able to obtain during your little network session. After that your dispatch will tell you how to proceed.

Chapter Questions

1. B:C fire extinguishers are only effective on

a) Tire fires
b) Electrical fires and burning liquids
c) Cloth, oil, and grease fires
d) The demon that live in manual transmission engines

2. If the cargo is on fire you should

a) Open the doors wide
b) Keep driving
c) Keep the doors shut
d) Spray the outside of the trailer

3. It takes the human body __ many hours to get rid of four drinks of alcohol

a) 2
b) 4
c) 3
d) Cold coffee

4. If you are prescribed a new drug:

a) Ask the doctor how it will impact your driving
b) Don't drive for a week
c) Tell your boss
d) Just say no

5. If you are too sick to drive

a) Keep driving to your next stop
b) Pullover and call your boss
c) Pullover and call 9-1-1
d) Puke out the window

6. It takes __ seconds for a combination vehicle to clear a single train track:

a) 2
b) 30
c) 14
d) Over 9,000

7. Brake Fade

a) Is normal wear on the brakes
b) Is caused when your brakes heat up from overuse
c) Isn't anything to worry about
d) Can happen anywhere

8. If you are obliged to leave the road, return by

a) Turning slowly and carefully
b) Making a quick sharp turn onto the road
c) Getting fully off the road and approaching at a 90-degree angle
d) Magic

9. Texting while driving has a federal fee of:

a) $2.70
b) $27.00
c) $270.00
d) $2,750.00

10. If you get into an accident remember:

a) S.O.R.E
b) P.A.I.N.S.
c) O.U.C.H.
d) N.E.D.M.

11. What is a retarder?

a) A device that can help slow your vehicle without the need for brakes
b) Medicines to prevent drowsiness
c) A tool for disperse the force of impact in the event of an accident
d) None of the above

Chapter Answers

1. b)
2. c)
3. b)
4. a)
5. c)
6. c)
7. b)
8. b)
9. d)
10. b)
11. a)

General Information Part 4: Transporting Cargo

The entire point of passing your CDL test is to get a job moving things from point A to point B with a really big vehicle. As you can imagine, there are many questions in the test that focus on how to move them.

Definitions

Here's some loading specific terminology you will need to know:

- **Gross Vehicle Weight (GVW):** This is the total amount of weight of a single vehicle inclusive of its load.
- **Gross Combination Weight (GCW):** The total amount of weight of a combination of vehicles inclusive of load.
- **Gross Vehicle Weight Rating (GVWR):** The value that is specified by the manufacturer as the fully loaded weight of a single vehicle.
- **Gross Combination Weight Rating (GCWR):** The specified value by the manufacturer as the loaded weight of a combination (articulated) vehicle.
- **Axle Weight:** The weight that is transferred to the ground by 1 axle or one axle set.
- **Tire Load:** The maximum weight a tire safely hauls at one given pressure. This value is indicated on the side of every tire.
- **Suspension Systems:** Suspension systems have a weight capacity value set by the manufacturer.
- **Coupling Device Capacity:** Coupling devices are classified by the maximum amount of weight they can pull and/or haul.

Cargo

Here are some other things you're going to need to know for the test:

- After initial inspection stop and inspect the cargo within the first 50 miles to adjust as needed.
- Re-Check your cargo at every break in the trip, and every three hours or 150 miles.
- Before setting out make sure you are aware of all federal, state, and local regulations for your route.
- Overloading vehicles affects steering, braking, speed control, stopping distance, and increasing strain on brakes.

Front Axles

Axels are very complicated for the purposes of the CDL test because they are critical to proper weight balance. Here's what you need to know.

- Excessive weight on the steering axle may cause difficulties with steering and damage to the axle and tires.
- Under-loaded *front* axles can result in too little on the *driving* axles and cause poor traction.

Yes, those are three separate axles we just referred to. It's confusing, but you need to know it. Sorry.

Loading Cargo

Put the weight in the center, and make sure there are wheels at each end of whatever you're towing. There, you now know everything about loading cargo onto a flatbed or trailer.

Securing Cargo

This pertains mostly to flatbeds but securing cargo is also important for closed trailers, especially if you're transporting any hazardous materials.

- Every piece of cargo requires at least two tie-downs.
- Federal regulation requires the cumulative working load limit of whichever fastener is used to secure an item or group of items against movement must be at least 1/2 times the weight of the article or group of articles. (Basically, whatever you use as a tie-down has to be able to hold twice the weight of whatever it's holding because stuff is going to be moving around as you drive.)
- Proper tie-down equipment must be used, including straps, ropes, chains, and high-tension devices such as winches, ratchets and cinching components. (A background in construction or BDSM is helpful here.)
- All tie-downs must be secured to the vehicle correctly using hooks, bolts, rails, or rings.
- You must have at least one tie-down in place for every ten feet of cargo.

Header Boards

While tie-downs are designed to protect and secure the cargo, header boards are there to protect you. They're like the headboard on a bed, only they keep whatever's on the truck bed from flying through your back window when you have to make an emergency stop.

Covering Cargo

Covering cargo with a tarp serves two purposes. It protects the cargo from the weather, and protects people from spilled cargo. Just make sure you check with state laws along your route pertaining to covering cargo. It is against federal law to let your cargo scatter litter on the highway. All cargo must be sealed to prevent spillage. There are only two types of litter allowed to be disbursed from your vehicle as it travels along the freeway: clear water, and feathers from live birds. So if you're transporting the world's first amphibious chickens it's open top all the way.

Cargo Needing Special Attention

Some cargo requires a little extra precaution no matter what kind of vehicle you're driving.

Dry Bulk

Bulk items are commonly stacked as high as possible in a trailer, and thus have a high center of gravity that can shift during turns or curves. You'd be surprised how much even a full load of toilet paper can affect your vehicle.

Livestock

They're living weights that can wander around causing unexpected shifts. If your livestock is in less than a full load, use bulkheads to keep the animals in designated areas. You need to keep them from congregating on one side and causing a rollover with a bovine rebellion.

Oversized Loads

These loads require extra lights, signs, warning flags, and the memeable "wide load" sticker. Such loads may also require a police escort or pilot vehicles to drive ahead of you. Check your state CDL handbook for specifics on required special markings for oversized loads, and be sure to check the requirements of any other states along your route before you head out.

Chapter Questions

1. Axle Weight is:

a) The weight of one axle
b) How much the axle can bare
c) The weight transferred to the ground by 1 axle or a set of axles
d) About 15 lbs

2. After the initial inspection, stop and inspect your cargo within the first 50 miles to:

a) Adjust as needed
b) Check it's still there
c) Steal some
d) Take inventory

3. If you under-load the front axle:

a) The other axles will get jealous
b) The driving axles will have poor traction
c) The steering axles will have poor rotation
d) The depressed axles will have poor self-esteem

4. All you need to know about loading cargo is put wheels at each end, and:

a) Just throw it in there
b) Heaviest on top
c) Put the weight in the center
d) Never trust a panda bear

5. Every piece of cargo must have:

a) A label
b) At least 2 tie-downs
c) A purpose
d) An address

6. Covering cargo protects the cargo from the weather and ___ from spills

a) People
b) The vehicle
c) You
d) Yo Mama

7. Which of these is not considered cargo needing special attention?

a) Dry Bulk
b) Livestock
c) Oversized Loads
d) Empty Containers

8. Header Boards protect:

a) You
b) The environment
c) Other drivers
d) Yo Mama again!

9. Proper tie-down equipment includes:

a) super glue and duct tape
b) ropes, chains and straps
c) twine, zip ties and belts
d) several hundred feet of yellow yarn

10. Livestock should be separated with bulkheads to prevent

a) Them tipping over the trailer
b) Escape
c) Messes in the trailer
d) World domination

11. How many tie- downs should have each piece of cargo?

a) 4
b) 1
c) At least two
d) 6

Chapter Answers

1. c)
2. a)
3. b)
4. c)
5. b)
6. a)
7. d)
8. a)
9. b)
10. a)
11. c)

Air Brakes

An air brake system is really three separate systems all working together.

- The service brake system
- The parking brake system
- The emergency brake system

When we talk about the emergency brake system, we are talking about a device that uses parts of both the service and parking brakes, but does not use air pressure to brake. It is a backup for when the air brake system fails. I say "when" and not "if" because air brakes are notorious for failure due to the high maintenance required to maintain them. They'll save your life though, so they're worth the time and effort. Here's what you need to know about air brakes for the test:

- When using air brakes, pressing the brake pedal causes compressed air to enter the brake chambers.
- Fluid commonly collects in compressed air tanks, which can freeze and cause your brakes to fail, so you should drain your tanks at the end of every work day if your system does not do it automatically.
- S-cams are used to apply the brakes and are called such because they are shaped like the letter "S."
- Heavy vehicles most commonly use S-cam brakes as foundation brakes for air brake systems.
- Be aware of your brake lag distance as it causes your air brakes to have a longer stopping distance than your regular hydraulic brakes.
- Your brake pedal is connected to the service brake system, which is separate from the emergency and parking brake systems.
- The stab braking method works with hydraulic and air brakes.
- If you are driving 55 mph on dry pavement, air brakes will add a brake lag of 32 feet to your total stopping distance. (There is some incomprehensible reason why this question comes up a lot, but not what the actual formula is. Probably because it's extremely complicated.)
- Some vehicles have alcohol evaporators designed to reduce the risk of ice building up inside the brake valves.
- Spring brakes, also known as emergency brakes, are controlled by the emergency brake lever and do not use air pressure to stop.
- Spring brakes are engaged manually using a toggle type control usually found on the dashboard.
- Do *not* use the brake pedals when the spring brakes are engaged.
- Spring brake power depends on the adjustment of service brakes.
- Air compressors will stop pumping air into the tanks at 125 psi which is a full charge for most systems.
- At 150 psi most vehicle's safety valves open to vent excessive pressure.
- Overheating the service brakes with excessive use can lead to the brake drums expanding. (Which is bad!)
- The low warning light for the air pressure gauge must kick on if the pressure drops below 60 psi, which is around half of a full charge for most systems.

- If you should see the low air pressure light come on, do not ignore it. Stop your truck as soon as possible in a safe place and have your air brake system checked as soon as possible.
- Converter dollies with anti-lock brake systems are required by law to have a yellow lamp on the left side.

Yeah, that last bullet point seems kind of random, but it'll make sense when we get to double and triple trailers.

Pre-Trip Air Brake Check

All air brakes lose pressure over time whether they are engaged or not. To check the rate of static air leakage, wait until the pressure gauge maximum pressure, then shut off the engine, then release the parking brake and let the system settle. Wait a minute and then check again the pressure gauge. The pressure should not have dropped any lower than:

- Two psi for single-vehicles
- Three psi for a combination of 2 vehicles
- Five psi for a combination of 3 or more vehicles

That may look a little confusing, but that's how it's likely going to look on the test. Just remember that a trailer is counted as a separate vehicle for the purposes of air brake systems.

Check your brake drums for cracks. Any cracking should be reported immediately, but if you notice a crack longer than half an inch do not attempt to operate the vehicle. It won't end well for you, and it probably won't be good for anybody who happens to be in front of you either.

Spring Brakes

While air brakes are effective, they're not the most reliable invention. As a precaution to this, all vehicles with air brakes have mechanical spring brakes built in as well. Spring brakes are held back by the air pressure of the air brakes, so they *should* kick in automatically when the air pressure drops too low.

It's best practice to switch over manually whenever the low pressure warning light pops up, but it's important test the automatic engagement as part of your pre-trip check. You can test that by continuing the step on and off the brakes until the parking brake valve pops out and the psi reduces enough to let the spring brakes to engage.

Dual Air Brake Systems

Since they are so prone to failure, some vehicles use a dual air brake system. These systems use a primary and a secondary system. Each system controls either the front or rear axles, but they are both controlled by the same brake controls. This means the front and back wheels have separate systems, but it's all controlled by the same pedal.

Slack Adjusters

S-cam brakes, called so because they are shaped like the letter S, are the most common type of foundation brakes used in air brake systems. The air pressure controls the S-cams, and the S-cams stop the wheels. You'll need to check your S-Cam brakes during pre-inspection. To do this, first make sure you're parked on completely level ground and put on a pair of heavy duty gloves. Release the parking brakes and find the slack adjusters for your vehicle. You'll probably have to consult your vehicle's user guide to find them the first time.

With your gloves on, give those slack adjusters a good hard pull. If you manage to move them more than an inch they need some adjustment. Too much slack in the adjusters means your vehicle will be hard to stop. Get your vehicle to a garage and get those adjusters adjusted ASAP!

Some other facts about slack adjusters you'll need to know for the test:

- All vehicles constructed since 1994 feature automatic slack adjusters, however, they are still prone to wear and must be checked manually.
- Most problems connected to slack adjusters either come from related brake components, or the adjusters being improperly installed to begin with.
- Automatic slack adjusters are produced by different manufacturers and they don't all work the same way. It is best not mix and match from competitive manufacturers.

One last word of advice for these things. Since loose slack adjusters are usually a sign of a much bigger underlying problem, get your vehicle to a skilled, certified mechanic and have it thoroughly checked out. Do not adjust it yourself and call it a day. That's like treating a brain hemorrhage with a Band-Aid.

Chapter Questions

1. **Air Brakes are:**

a) Always effective
b) Dangerous
c) Uncommon
d) Notorious for failure

2. **S-Cams:**

a) Are shaped like an H
b) Are cameras that help you see around the vehicle
c) Are used to apply the breaks
d) Are uncommon in heavy vehicles

3. **Some vehicles have alcohol evaporators to:**

a) Let you get drunk on the road
b) Keep you sober on the road
c) Fool D.U.I. tests
d) Keep the air tanks from freezing

4. **Spring Brakes:**

a) Do not use air pressure
b) Are also known as emergency brakes
c) Should automatically engage if the air pressure drops too low
d) All of the above

5. **When testing the static air leak of a single vehicle, the pis should not drop by more than _ in one minute.**

a) 2
b) 3
c) 5
d) 10

6. **Dual air brake systems are controlled by**

a) The emergency brake
b) The brake pedal
c) The brake pedal and the emergency brake
d) Pure will power

7. **Automatic slack adjusters:**

a) Are required for all vehicles built after 1994
b) Never need to be adjusted
c) Can be tested without gloves
d) Can be mixed and matched with competitive manufacturers safely

8. **If a slack adjuster is loose it's usually a sign of**

a) Your impending doom
b) Your vehicle needs an oil change
c) A bigger underlying problem
d) Nothing you need to worry about

9. **At 150 psi most vehicles:**

a) Vent excessive pressure
b) Are under pressure
c) Are at adequate pressure
d) Explode

10. **You should not use the brake pedals while the spring brakes are engaged:**

a) True
b) False
c) Bannana
d) Answer c is misspelled

11. **At how many psi does the air compressor usually stop pumping air into the tanks?**

a) 145 psi
b) 150 psi
c) 155 psi
d) 160 psi

Chapter Answers

1. d)
2. c)
3. d)
4. d)
5. a)
6. b)
7. a)
8. c)
9. a)
10. a)
11. b)

Combination Vehicles

This is what you typically tend to think of when you first think of trucking. A combination vehicle is a truck or tractor with a trailer or flatbed attached to the back.
Here's what you need to know:

- Always steer gently.
- Always approach any turn with extreme caution and take it slowly.
- The "crack-the-whip" effect is caused by reward amplification, and occurs when you make quick turns and is where the trailer receives significantly stronger force during a turn, drastically increasing the chance of a roll over.
- Reward amplification is doubled for a single trailer combination vehicle, three and a half times for double trailers, and five times triple trailers.
- Sum up second to your following distance for every ten feet of your vehicle's total length, plus another second whenever you break 40 mph.
- Railroad crossings can be particularly dangerous for combination vehicles since they are especially prone to snagging on the tracks as you cross.
- The most at risk vehicles when crossing a railroad are low slung units and single-axle tractors.
- If you get caught on railroad tracks, call 9-1-1 immediately and provide them with any identifiable landmarks including the railroad's DOT number if available.
- Combination vehicles without trailers attached to them are often referred to as "bobtail trucks" and they are even harder to stop than vehicles with fully loaded trailers behind them! (Physics is weird.)
- Always brake early and smoothly, sudden stops or movements can cause your trailers to "jackknife."

Combination Vehicle Safety

Fully loaded rigs have a higher center of gravity and are 10 times more likely to suffer a rollover during any kind of accident. According to the CDL handbook there are two ways to reduce the risk of rollovers in combination vehicles:

- Keep the load the closest possible to the ground
- Always make turns slowly and brake gradually

Low cargo means a lower center of gravity, which means rollovers are *slightly* less likely to occur. It's not much, but it's better than a guaranteed catastrophe.
Controlling your speed is always your best bet to prevent a rollover. Newton's second law says Force = Mass x Acceleration. Force is what's going to kill you, and acceleration is the only thing you have any real control over once you get on the road, so exercise as much control over it as possible.
Even if you don't rollover immediately, sudden braking or turns can cause your trailer to "Jackknife." Jackknifing is where the trailer or trailers swing out to the side, often while braking or turning. This turns everything you're towing into a gigantic mace capable of destroying other vehicles, your vehicle, anything

around your vehicle, and since it destroys the trailer you're probably going to have some pretty hefty littering fines to deal with. If you survive the crash that is.

Combination Vehicle Air Brakes

- The hand valve specifically controls the trailer brakes and should only be used to test the trailer brakes during inspection. Do not use the hand valve while driving. It can cause the trailer to skid and overturn your vehicle. Your brake pedal safely controls all the brakes at the same time so only use that.
- Never use the hand valve to park a combination vehicle. That's what the parking brake is for. If you use the hand valve the air inside will leak over time and the brakes will lose pressure and you will have no brakes at all.
- Some newer vehicles come with air supply control specifically for controlling the air brakes in the trailer. If your vehicle is provided with one, you should see a red eight-sided knob inside the cabin. It looks a little like a stop sign.
- Every air supply control works the same way. Pulling out the knob shuts off the air supply and engages the trailer's emergency brakes. Pushing it in again lets the air flow back into the trailer air brakes.
- If the pressure in the trailer air brakes drops below a certain psi the trailer's emergency brakes should kick on. However, this can be anywhere from 20-45 psi depending on the vehicle.

Trailer Air Lines

There are two new airlines you need to be aware of when it comes to combination vehicles: The Service Air Line, and the Emergency Air line. The service airline is pretty simple as it's controlled by the brake pedal, but the emergency air line is a little more complicated.

It controls the pressure to the air tanks and the emergency brakes. If air pressure is lost to the emergency line of the trailer then emergency brakes will engage. This is so that if the trailer rips free from your vehicle on the road, the emergency brakes will kick on and stop it from continuing down the road out of control. Of course their line can also lose pressure while it's still attached, which doesn't bode well for the vehicle trying to pull it.

Fortunately emergency lines are color coded as red so you can easily see them during checks.

Backing Up with a Trailer

If you ever thought parallel parking was a pain in the butt, buy yourself some hemorrhoid cream and get ready to suffer. The good thing is that once you know how to do it properly, you're unlikely to forget. It's a bit like riding a bike, just with even more screamed obscenities.

Step 1: Set Yourself up For Success

While it's a good rule for life in general, it's especially important when backing up a trailer. Try your very best to line yourself up so that you can back up in a straight line towards your target. If you must back up on a curve, back towards the driver side so you can see what you're doing.

Step 2: Check your Path

Unless you're part giraffe there is no way for you to physically see the entire path your vehicle is going to take from the driver's seat. Even if you have back up cameras there are still plenty of blind spots that can hide any number of dangers. Anything from potholes to kamikaze porcupines could be waiting in your path, and unless you get out of the vehicle (don't forget the keys and the parking brake), and walk around it and along your entire path, you'll have no way of knowing about the hidden dangers.

Yes it will probably take a couple of minutes and you were over this stupid job fifty miles ago, but now is not the time to get lazy! Take it from experience, you will *never* live down crashing right at the finish line. Or running over a porcupine.

Step 3: Back Up Slow and Keep Checking

You cannot back up slowly enough! You want to keep the trailer (or lord forbid, *trailers*) as straight as possible. The instant you notice a trailer start to veer off *S.A.C.* it.

Stop the vehicle:

You should be traveling very slow enough that a quick stop won't have any adverse effect. If you are backing up fast enough that you can't stop quickly then you are doing it wrong!

Assess the situation:

Check both of your mirrors and get out of the vehicle again. If the trailer is drifting off center then there's a reason, and you're not going to be able to correct it until you know what it is.

Correct the problem:

If you only have one trailer, then you should be able to counter steer as you back up to correct it. If you have more than one trailer you're likely going to buckle them if you try to keep backing up. It's better to pull forward instead to straighten the trailers out, though again, do it very slowly.

Hose Couplers

Hose couplers, also known as glad hands (for some reason), are what connect the air lines from the vehicle to the trailer. When connecting glad hands make sure to clean the rubber seals first to ensure that no air will escape through the connection point. Press the two seals together with couplers at a 90 degree angle to each other, and then turn the hand attached to the hose to lock the couplers together.

To put it in simpler terms, clean off the ends and attach the hose to the nozzle like you would any other compressed air hose.

If there isn't a trailer to connect to, there should be either dummy couplers to attach the hoses too, or the glad hands may lock together. Do not let the hoses dangle as they can become damaged or dirty.

There should be two colors for the air lines: red for emergency lines, and blue for supply lines. They may also have the words "service" and "emergency" stamped on them as well, but it's not uncommon for them to not. If you cross these lines the emergency brakes for the trailer may not disengage, however it's not a guarantee. Older trailers do not have separate emergency brakes, and if you cross the lines then you will be able to move, but you won't have any trailer brakes. In the words of Egon Spengler, "Don't cross the streams. It would be bad." (Reltman, 1984)

Chapter Questions

1. You should steer combination vehicles:

a) Harshly
b) Gently
c) Like a boat
d) Like a rock

2. The Crack-whip-effect is caused by:

a) Reward amplification
b) Penalty gratification
c) Ambrosial indignation
d) Bob

3. Bobtail trucks are:

a) Tucks without trailers
b) Trucks that bounce a lot
c) A specific brand of truck
d) A cute hairstyle

4. Railroad crossings can be particularly dangerous for combination vehicles since:

a) They are especially prone to snagging
b) They are very long
c) The train gods hate them most of all
d) They have reckless drivers

5. Jackknifing is when:

a) The trailer or trailers swing out to the side
b) You feel road rage on the way to a sword convention
c) You abandon the trailer in the middle of the highway
d) A 1984 movie starring Daniel Quade

6. Step 1 of backing up with a trailer is to:

a) Set yourself up for success
b) Check your path
c) Back Up Slowly
d) Hunt down the porcupine queen

7. A high center of gravity:

a) Makes turns more dangerous
b) Helps you keep balance
c) Helps you on downhill trips
d) Doesn't affect your driving

8. You should never use the hand valve to park a combination vehicle:

a) True
b) False
c) Bannanna
d) Answer c is misspelled again

9. There are ___ new airlines on a commercial vehicle compared to other vehicles with air brakes.

a) 2
b) 4
c) 6
d) 8

10. The instant you notice a trailer starts to veer off while backing up ___ it.

a) S.A.C.
b) B.A.G.
c) T.A.G.
d) S.H.A.G.

11. How are Hose Couplers also known?

a) Glad hands
b) Packers
c) Sealers
d) Lockers

12. When you back up

a) Do not make movements longer than 3 seconds before stopping
b) Turn off the radio to increase concentration
c) You should be traveling very slow enough that a quick stop won't have any adverse effect
d) None of the above

Chapter Answers

1. b)
2. a)
3. a)
4. a)
5. a)
6. a)
7. a)
8. a)
9. a)
10. a)
11. a)
12. c)

Doubles and Triples

What's worse than one unwieldy profanity inducing attachment? Two or three of the things! There isn't much difference between one, two or three trailers. Everything is just three to five times more dangerous. Here's what you need to know:

- Improper coupling and uncoupling of trailers is extremely dangerous.
- The last trailer in the line is the one most likely to rollover. (Watch your butt!)
- You should load the heaviest trailer closest to the main vehicle, and the lightest the furthest from it. This is to help with that rollover tendency I just mentioned.
- If the second trailer doesn't have spring breaks do the following:
    - Start the vehicle
    - Check that all lines into the trailer are closed
    - Connect the emergency line to charge the trailer air tank
    - Disconnect the emergency line once the air tank is fully charged

Coupling and Uncoupling

This is where most of the unique problems with doubles and triple trailers come from, as well as the majority of the unique test questions, and almost all of it revolves around your new friend the converter dolly.
The CDL handbook defines a converter dolly as: a coupling device of 1 or 2 axles and a fifth-wheel with which to couple a semi-trailer to the back of a tractor-trailer combination forming a double bottom rig.
It's basically a female to male plug adapter for trailers, and about 99.99% of the ones you encounter are going to be finicky as hell.

Coupling with Converter Dollies

Step 1

Make sure that the landing gear for the trailer you're going to attach the converter dolly to is down and secure. Even an empty trailer can easily turn a human hand into you-flavored jelly.

Step 2

Release the brakes on the dolly so you can move it around. If it has spring breaks, use the dolly parking brake control. If it has air brakes, open the air tank petcock. No, I do not know what a petcock is. I'm not googling it and neither should you. Just find a valve somewhere on the thing and open it until it moves.

Step 3

Wheel the dolly into place by hand and position it in line with the kingpin on the trailer.
Or, if the dolly is too far away from the trailer and you don't feel like pushing it the whole way:

1. Position the combination as closely as possible to the converter dolly.

2. Move the dolly to the rear of the first semi-trailer and couple it with the trailer.
3. Lock the pintle hook.
4. Position the dolly support in the raised position.
5. Move the dolly next to the nose of the second trailer, as close as possible.
6. Lower the dolly support.
7. Disengage the dolly from the first trailer.

And *then* wheel the dolly into place by hand and position it in line with the kingpin on the trailer.

Step 4

Now that you've got the dolly in place on the front of the second trailer, back up the first trailer to it and lock the pintle hook in place. The pintle hook is the thing that actually connects the two trailers.

Step 5

Now we need to connect the converter dolly to the front of the second trailer. If you're confused, remember that the previous steps were all just to line the dolly up with the trailer.

- Make sure the trailer brakes are locked in place and chock the wheels of the second trailer so it can't move.
- Check that the second trailer is slightly lower than the center of the "fifth-wheel" on the converter dolly. You want the trailer to raise up slightly when the converter dolly is pushed under it.
- Raise the landing gear just slightly off the ground. This is to prevent the landing gear from being damaged if the trailer moves during the coupling.
- Get back in the vehicle and slowly back the converter dolly under the second trailer until they connect.
- Exit from the vehicle and inspect coupling by pulling against the pin of the second semitrailer.
- Do a visual inspection of the coupling. No gap should be between the upper and lower fifth-wheel, and the locking jaws of the connector dolly are closed on the kingpin of the trailer.
- Once you're sure the coupling is secure, connect the safety chains, air hoses, and light cords as normal.
- If the converter dolly has air brakes, close the converter dolly air tank petcock and close the valves on the back of the second trailer. Then open the shut-off valves at the rear of the first trailer and the dolly. (You're making the air flow into the second trailer without it going out the other end.)
- Raise the landing gear up completely and get back in the cabin.

Now that that's all done, charge the trailer brakes by pushing the "air supply" knob in, and monitor the presence of air in the rear of the second trailer by opening the emergency line shut-off. If the air pressure isn't building up then something is wrong. Do not attempt to drive the vehicle like this. If the trailer brakes don't work you're just asking for a rollover.

Uncoupling with Converter Dollies

Now we do most of the same thing, just in reverse.

- Park your vehicle in a straight line on firm level ground. Do not attempt to uncouple on any level of grade if you can help it.
- Activate the parking brakes and lock the wheels of the second trailer.
- Lower the second trailer's landing gear enough to take the weight off the converter dolly enough to be removed.
- Close the air shut-off valves on the trailer and the converter dolly if applicable and disconnect all lines from the second trailer and secure them properly.
- Release the dolly brakes followed by the fifth-wheel latch.
- Get back in the vehicle and slowly pull the first trailer forward until the attached dolly slides free from the second trailer.
- Get back out of the vehicle and lower the converter dolly's landing gear.
- Apply the brake and chock the wheels of the converter dolly. (The thing is heavy enough to damage something if it starts rolling.)
- Release the pintle hook still connecting the converter dolly to the first trailer.
- Remove the chocks and carefully pull the dolly clear, making sure no lines are still attached or tangled.

And there's everything you need to know about converter dollies. Coupling and uncoupling a third dolly is the exact same process, though I should point out that several states do not allow triple trailers due to how dangerous they are. Always check the laws of any state you may travel through.

Though if I may offer some personal advice, if a company requires you to pull a triple trailer, find another job. Don't be charmed by how much they might sweeten the deal, your safety is not that employer's concern.

Chapter Questions

1. Improper coupling and uncoupling of trailers is

a) Bad but not terrible
b) Extremely Dangerous
c) Potentially problematic
d) Not something you should tell your parents

2. Most of the problems unique to double and triple trailers revolve around the:

a) Axle
b) Converter Dolly
c) Driver
d) The train gods

3. There are _ steps to uncoupling a trailer

a) 5
b) 10
c) 15
d) 20

4. Make sure the landing gear is __ if you are going to attach the converter dolly:

a) Up
b) Down
c) Detached
d) Attached

5. All of the answers the previous questions are:

a) C
b) A
c) D
d) B

6. Is it possible that there are more than 2 dollies connected to your vehicle?

a) Yes
b) No

7. Get back out of the vehicle and lower the converter dolly's landing gear is:

a) What every truck driver should do when he wakes up
b) One of the steps of uncoupling with converter dollies
c) None of the above
d) All of the above

Chapter Answers

1. b)
2. b)
3. b)
4. b)
5. d)
6. a)
7. b)

Tank Vehicles

No, your commercial driver's license will not permit you to drive an M4 Sherman down the interstate. The tanks we're talking about here are the sort you store liquids and gasses in. You know, the kind that usually explodes in action movies.

Maybe the M4 would be safer...

The good news is that a tank vehicle is pretty much just a combination vehicle. All the same rules apply, all the same cautions about taking turns and braking slowly and gradually, everything about air brakes, coupling and uncoupling, doubles and triples, it's all the same.

Except for a few little details that, surprise, make them even harder to control and more dangerous!

Here are some things you'll need to know for the test:

- Keep steady pressure on the brakes as you slow down, and try not to start moving again just after stopping. The sloshing effect can affect your acceleration.
- Brake well in advance before a stop and increase your following distance.
- If you must perform a quick stop to avoid an accident, use controlled or stab braking. (It won't help much honestly, but at least you'll feel like you're doing something.)
- Slow down when taking a curve and then accelerate *slightly* as you move through it.
- The maximum driving time in a single working period is 10 hours for drivers of tank vehicles with a capacity of over 500 gallons when transporting flammable liquids. (You are legally required to only work semi-decent hours if you can explode.)
- Baffled liquid tanks have bulkheads with holes in them to allow the liquid to flow through at a controlled pace. However, they do not protect against side-to-side surges that can occur when taking a turn.
- Unbaffled liquid tanks, also called "smooth bore" tanks, are most commonly used to transport food products due to sanitation requirements.

Surges

Your first problem with driving a tank vehicle is the high center of gravity. This is true of nearly every commercial vehicle, but the danger is amplified to the extreme due to your cargo often being liquids.

Liquids are like toddlers on a sugar rush, they are physically incapable of sitting still even when you desperately want to stop. Every movement of the tank is echoed and amplified by the sloshing of the liquid inside. While this is dangerous enough in optimal conditions, on slippery roads the sloshing effect can actually throw your souped-up rig around like a rowboat caught in the tide.

The obvious way to fix this problem would be to fill the tank up to the brim to give the liquid as little room to move about in as possible. But, there are two issues with this idea. The first is that liquids are some of the densest forms of matter, and therefore the heaviest. You can easily exceed legal weight limits for a tank just by filling it only part way.

The other problem is that as liquids warm up from sloshing around, or being in a metal tank in the hot sun all day, they expand and increase the pressure inside the tank. You can *never* fill a tank of any liquid completely full. The pressure would cause the tank to rupture, potentially turning your trailer into a time bomb.

Every liquid you will be transporting has what's called an outage requirement, which tells you how much empty space you must leave in the tank. In addition to the outage limit of the liquid, there are other limits on how much you can fill the tank trailer for other reasons, though these can vary from state to state.

Here's a brief list of the more common factors you'll need to take into account, at least as it relates to the test:

- The weight of the liquid
- Legal weight limits of all roads and bridges along your route and potential detours
- The temperature of the load and weather along your route

Bulkheads

For any of you like me who are not nautically inclined, a bulkhead is a divider inside a tank that keeps liquid separated. This helps a lot with weight distribution and helps keep the liquid more contained without overfilling. An important warning you should keep in mind both for the test and when actually driving, is not to let too much weight settle in one bulkhead. This most commonly happens during travel over a steep grade, so take a break to let the liquid settle in place after you get over one.

Chapter Questions

1. Baffled liquid tanks:

a) Have Bulkheads with holes in them
b) Have Solid Bulkheads
c) Are used mostly for food products
d) Are very confused

2. Slow down when taking a curve and then

a) Accelerate slightly as you move through it
b) Continue to slow down as you move through it
c) Floor it as you move through it
d) Close your eyes and let the train gods take the wheel

3. Surges is:

a) A caffeinated soft drink from the 90s
b) When your vehicle has a sudden burst of speed
c) When the liquid moves inside the tank due to a turn or stop
d) Helpful with braking

4. You should never fill up liquid take to the brim:

a) True
b) False
c) Banaana
d) Seriously what is with c?

5. Which, among the 4 alternatives below, does not qualify as a common factor for how much liquid you can put in a tank?

a) The weight of the liquid
b) Legal weight limits of all roads and bridges
c) How many bulkheads the tank has
d) The temperature of the load

6. What does the outage requirement indicate?

a) This word does not exist
b) How much empty space you must leave in the tank
c) The maximum transportable weight of that liquid
d) How many times can you carry the same type of load within the same tank

7. Why should you never fill the tank all the way up?

a) Because the liquids you carry could expand during transport causing a spillage, and you may exceed the allowed weight limit
b) I should always fill my tank to the maximum to maximize my efforts
c) I don't know
d) None of the above

Chapter Answers

1. a)
2. a)
3. c)
4. a)
5. c)
6. b)
7. a)

Hazardous Materials

I will begin by either disappointing you or giving you an intense feeling of relief.

If you are reading this book, there's a good chance you don't need to, and likely shouldn't even try to take the Hazardous Materials Endorsement Test for the CDL.

If you are studying to get your first CDL license then you have no business trying to drive HazMat. If you are an expert driver who is looking to expand their opportunities please skip to the "Further Study" chapter at the back of the book. Also I hope you enjoyed the other sections.

Because of the dangerous nature of HazMat transportation, no trustworthy employer will hire anyone with anything less than a full year of commercial driving experience. If you do find an employer who is willing to hire a greenhorn to transport extremely dangerous materials across state lines, kindly thank them for their time, inform them that you'll be in touch, and get the hell out of there. They were probably going to use you as a pawn in some nefarious insurance scheme you wouldn't survive to collect on.

Since hazardous materials can kill not only you, but everyone around you, and everyone that might have come within smelling distance of your vehicle, there are a lot of rules and regulations surrounding how to load, transport, and unload this stuff. Enough to fill a whole other book in fact!

While we will not be covering everything you need to know for the HazMat endorsement test, there is some information you should know for your own safety, especially since you'll still be handling HazMat without an endorsement.

The remaining part of this chapter will be dedicated to what you need to know for the general knowledge test as well as some helpful information for how to not kill yourself.

Here's some of the things you'll need to keep in mind:

- Make sure the shipper identified, marked, and labeled the HazMat properly.
- Refuse any leaking packages or shipments.
- Always check if placards are required for the shipment and affix them to all four sides of the vehicle before you leave the facility. (You won't actually, but that's a test question.)
- Safely transport shipments without delay. (Some HazMat material can be time-sensitive in addition to temperature-sensitive.)
- Know and follow all special rules about transporting the class of HazMat you are carrying.
- Ensure that all HazMat shipping papers are certified by the original shipper.
- Report all incidents and accidents involving HazMat to the appropriate government agency, when the accident or incident occurs while the driver has physical control of the shipment. (Though you should probably report it even if you weren't in control.)
- You must keep HazMat shipping documents in or on:
    - A pouch on the driver's door
    - Clearly visible within immediate reach while the seat belt is fastened while driving
    - The driver's seat when outside the vehicle

What Kind of Hazmat Can You Transport Without a License?

We touched on this briefly at the end of the general knowledge chapter, but not all HazMat requires a HazMat endorsement to transport, but if the cargo does not require placards on the vehicle you do not require a HazMat endorsement to transport it.

So what kind of HazMat doesn't require placards?

To answer that question the federal government created two different classifications which are confusingly called Placard Table 1 and Placard Table 2.

If a material is on Placard Table 1 it requires placards in any amount and you can not transport it without a HazMat endorsement on your license.

If the material is on Placard Table 2, it does not require a placard *if* you are transporting less than 1,001 lbs. of Placard Table 2 materials in total, *and* the material in question does not have a secondary hazard that requires a "DANGEROUS WHEN WET" placard, or the words "INHALATION HAZARD" are on the shipping paper or the package, which require a "POISON GAS" or "POISON INHALATION" placard.

Confusing isn't it? Don't worry, even when you do get your HazMat license properly labeling HazMat material isn't your responsibility. You're only responsible for checking that it's been labeled correctly and holding others accountable.

PLACARD TABLE 1 ANY AMOUNT

If your vehicle contains any amount of…	Placard as…
1.1 Mass explosives	Explosives 1.1
1.2 Project Hazards	Explosives 1.2
1.3 Mass Fire Hazards	Explosives 1.3
2.3 Poisonous/toxic gases	Poison gas
4.3 Dangerous When Wet	Dangerous When Wet
5.2 (Organic peroxide, Type B, liquid or solid, temperature controlled)	Organic peroxide
6.1 (Inhalation hazard zone A & B only)	Poison/toxic inhalation
7 (Radioactive Yellow III label only)	Radioactive

PLACARD TABLE 2 1,000 POUNDS OR MORE

Category of material (hazard class or division number and additional description, as appropriate)	Placard Name
1.4 Minor explosion	Explosives 1.4
1.5 Very insensitive	Explosives 1.5
1.6 Extremely insensitive	Explosives 1.6
2.1 Flammable gases	Flammable gas
2.2 Non-flammable gases	Non-flammable gas
3 Flammable liquids	Flammable
Combustible liquid	Combustible*
4.1 Flammable solids	Flammable solid
4.2 Spontaneously combustible	Spontaneously combustible
5.1 Oxidizers	Oxidizer
5.2 (Other than organic peroxide, Type B, liquid or solid, temperature controlled)	Organic peroxide
6.1 (Other than inhalation hazard zone A or B)	Poison
6.2 Infectious substances	(None)
8 Corrosives	Corrosive
9 Miscellaneous HazMat	Class 9**
ORM-D	(None)

* FLAMMABLE may be used in place of a COMBUSTIBLE on a cargo tank or portable tank.
** Class 9 Placards are not required for domestic transportation.

Holding Others Accountable

One of your most important roles in HazMat, aside from transporting it safely, of course, is recognizing mislabels and holding others accountable. Catching other people's mistakes also happens to be really satisfying, so here's who is accountable for what.
Also, it is possible for this information to show up on the general knowledge exam.

The Shipper

The shipper is the person who sends the project out from manufacturing or refining. They're the first people who deal with HazMat cargo, and the ones in charge of correctly marking and recording it.
They are responsible for the following:

- ID number
- Proper shipping name
- Hazard Class
- Packing group
- Correct packaging
- Correct label and markings
- Correct placards (if applicable)

Once they've gotten all that taken care of, they certify the shipping papers and send them along to the carrier.

The Carrier

The carrier is basically you, but cooler. They transport the cargo by train, plane, or boat until it's time to pass it off to you. Most of their responsibility lies in checking the cargo to hold the shipper accountable, and transporting the cargo safely until they unload it at your pick-up facility. It's also their job to refuse any cargo that is improperly labeled or packed by the shipper.

Receipt of Cargo

Now that the cargo is in the same building as you, it's time for you to inspect it. Yes, the shipper and the carrier both already inspected it, but if someone dies, like you, it'll be your fault if you didn't catch the problem.
Check the package's marking and labels for the following:

- Make sure the name of the HazMat matches the name on the shipping paper
- Make sure the package includes the name and address of the shipper or consignee
- The HazMat shipping name and ID number are clearly visible on the package itself
- All additional required labels are present and clearly visible. This includes state, federal, and internationally required warnings labels, in all required languages.

Quick Fact List

Here are some final HazMat related things you're likely to see on the test:

- Never use burning devices such as flares or fuses around a tank filled with flammable liquids, gasses, or explosives.
- Be aware of any road restrictions along your route while transporting HazMat or waists.
- Do not smoke within 25 feet of any vehicle carrying Explosives, Flammable Liquids, Flammable Solids, Spontaneously combustible materials, or Oxidizers.
- Always turn your engine off before refueling a motor vehicle containing HazMat. (This is a question on the test, though I can't understand why anyone would fill up any vehicle with the motor on.)
- Don't park less than 300 feet from an open fire while transporting HazMat. (You shouldn't be parking that close anyway, but still.)
- Do not ever drive a placarded vehicle close to open fires unless you can pass safely without stopping. (It's not really relevant to you or the test, but it is an oddly weird and memorable law.)

Chapter Questions

1. This book will prep you for the HazMat Endorsement test and you should take it:

a) False
b) Wrong
c) Nope
d) All of the above

2. You should __ any packages or shipments that are leaking

a) Replace
b) Refuse
c) Reuse
d) Recycle

3. You must keep HazMat shipping papers in or on:

a) A pouch on the driver's door
b) In full view and within easy reach while driving
c) The driver's seat when he or she is out of the vehicle
d) It's all of the above I get it already! I get it!

4. What kind of HazMat can you transport without a HazMat endorsement?

a) None explosives
b) Anything without a placard
c) Waist
d) Live scorpions, but only green ones

5. The federal government created two different classifications for HazMat which are called:

a) Placard Table 1 and Placard Table 2
b) Placard Table A and Placard Table B
c) Hazardous and Non-Hazardous
d) Mike and Joe

6. Who is the first figure that handles an HazMat load?

a) You
b) The shipper
c) The recipient
d) The owner of the vehicle on which the cargo is shipped

7. Who is the carrier?

a) You
b) The one who transports the cargo by train, plane or ship until it is delivered to you
c) The one who takes the goods you transported to their destination
d) The legal owner of the vehicle on which the goods are transported

Chapter Answers

1. d)
2. b)
3. d)
4. b)
5. a)
6. b)
7. b)

Buses

Buses may not be what you typically think of when someone says "commercial vehicles", but they are the most common type. We've already covered most of the related material in the previous chapters, so here are the last few bus specific things.

Hazardous Materials on Busses

Most hazardous materials are not allowed on public busses. Which makes sense since buses are supposed to be for people. However, certain hazardous materials can be transported by bus under certain conditions. You will need to check your state CDL for what materials are allowed since it varies state to state.

It can also be quite an entertaining read. For example, in California it is technically legal to bring 100 lbs of arsenic, 100lbs of 9mm ammunition, 100lbs of sealed containers filled with helium, and 100lbs of raw uranium so long as it is properly packaged and you put it in the overhead compartment.

Passenger Supervision

Busses are perfect for people who can multitask or are part chameleon. Not only do you need to keep one eye on the road, but you also need one on the passengers behind you.

You are responsible for your passenger's safety, so make sure they keep the aisle clear, ensure all handicapped passengers are properly secured, and you have a full thermos of coffee and plenty of hand sanitizer for your break when the last walking germ farm gets off your bus.

If you have a disruptive passenger, remember that you are still responsible for their safety along with everyone else's. Kick them off the bus by all means, but don't do it anywhere that would be unsafe for them. The closest well lit area or scheduled bus stop will do.

Common Accidents

Bus accidents most frequently happen at intersections. This is because buses are much longer than average vehicles, and most bus drivers seem to think that because they operate on a schedule, stop signs and yellow lights do not apply to them.

It's also not uncommon for buses to lose some paint and mirrors to other vehicles as they pull out from a bus stop. In fact, busses are probably some of the most accident-prone vehicles on the road due to driver recklessness.

Remember, keeping your schedule is not worth getting into an accident. Just because the vehicle is owned by the city, doesn't mean you own the road.

Railroads and Drawbridges

The train gods are not merciful to busses. You are an imperfect imitation of their form and your presence is only barely tolerated.

- Stop between 15 and 50 feet before a railroad crossing.
- Watch and hear for trains in either direction. Open your forward door if necessary.
- If one train has already passed, wait and make sure that another train is not approaching from the other side as well.
- If you are cursed with a manual transmission, never change gears while crossing the tracks.

Drawbridges are oddly treacherous towards busses as well. When you are approaching one stop at least 50 feet away from the bridge and ensure that it is completely down before crossing.

There are a few exceptions to these rules, and you can proceed without stopping at railroad crossings and drawbridges if:

- There is an attendant or officer directing traffic
- It is a streetcar crossing
- There is a green traffic signal directly in front of or above the crossing or entrance
- The railroad crossing is marked as "exempt" or "abandoned" (If a bridge is marked that way however, do not cross it, and find an alternative route.)

After-Trip Vehicle Inspection

Once the last passenger is gone and you've pulled into the bus barn it's time to see what new damage the public has done to your transit. Mark any new or pre-existing defects and safety concerns on a written inspection report for the mechanics team. Pay special attention to any safety related parts such as handholds, seats, emergency exits, and windows. If there is no new damage, mark that as well since it's a small miracle and should be recorded for posterity.

Other Tips

- Avoid refueling your bus with passengers on board unless it is absolutely necessary.
- Never fueling in a closed building with people on board.
- Don't talk to riders or engaging in any other distracting activity while riding.
- Don't haul or push a disabled bus with people aboard the vehicle, unless getting off would be unsafe. (Such as the bus will explode if it drops below 50 mph.)

Chapter Questions

1. If you have a disruptive passenger you should have them leave at the nearest:

a) Safe place
b) Stop
c) City
d) Wherever

2. The most common bus accidents happen at:

a) Night
b) Small towns
c) Intersections
d) When your not looking

3. You cannot pass over a drawbridge without stopping if:

a) There is an attendant or officer directing traffic
b) It is a streetcar crossing
c) There is a green traffic signal directly in front of or above the crossing or entrance
d) The railroad crossing is marked as "exempt" or "abandoned"

4. During your after-trip inspection you must mark down any:

a) New damage
b) Existing damage
c) Lack of damage
d) All of the above

5. You never should refuel in a closed construction with passengers on board.

a) True
b) False
c) Banana
d) The question is asked ambiguously

6. In which case can you haul or push a bus with passengers on board?

a) Always
b) Never
c) Only when they offer you money to stay on board
d) Only if getting them off represents a danger

7. Which of the following options implies that you can cross a railroad crossing or drawbridge without stopping?

a) It is a streetcar crossing
b) You know well the train schedule
c) You are late
d) The driver before you did it

Chapter Answers

1. a)
2. c)
3. d)
4. d)
5. a)
6. d)
7. a)

Further Study

The Good News

Congratulations, you got to the final chapter! Eat some chocolate, have a drink, take a nap. You earned it! Just enjoy it while you can, because I'm afraid I've got some bad news waiting when you're done. Ready? You're sure? Okay.

The Bad News

If all you have done until this time is read this book, you're going to fail every portion of the CDL test. If you read the introduction this shouldn't come as a surprise to you, but I figured you might have forgotten somewhere around chapter four.

All the previous chapters were designed to catapult you into the world of commercial driving, but now it's time to teach you how to fly!

Or, drive as the case may be.

The Written Test Prep

Let's get the band-aid off and face the worst news. Do you recall when I said you to download a copy of your state's Commercial Drivers Handbook and take a look at how dry and wordy it was? Well, you're going to have to read it.

I know, it's a miserable fate and you probably bought this book in the hopes of avoiding it, but it's the only surefire way to make sure you get all the state-specific material. Plus, you don't have to read the whole thing! Just the sections you're going to be testing for. This book has already given you an easy introduction to all the basics.

Reading the chapters you need in the CDL handbook will also do miracles for your information retention. It's a weird phenomenon, but getting the same information from a second source really does help the human mind remember it better. Things you might have been a little foggy on are likely to click into place, and because the layout, phrasing, and tone of this book are all going to be different from the state handbook, your brain will be connecting dots instead of trying to process new concepts.

Bet you thought I was just a naturally charismatic writer, huh? Don't answer that.

The point is reading this guide and then the handbook one time each is roughly the same equivalent of reading through the handbook alone half a dozen times for the average reader. There are of course exceptions, people with photographic memories and such, but slightly altered repetition is one of the most successful study techniques of the 21st century.

Of course I'm not just asking you to take my word for it. If you want to see your level of progress there's an easy way to do it: practice tests.

Practice Tests

Before you go shilling out any money on internet scams let me assure you that you need not spend a digital penny on anything to find reliable practice tests for everything on CDL tests. All you need to do is type "CDL general knowledge Practice Test" into google and you will be given a wide selection of practice tests to choose from.

Most websites use the old "first one's free" approach, and let you take at least one practice test from each section of the CDL without creating a login or offering up any of your information. I'd still recommend you use incognito mode or better yet Virtual Private Network (V.P.N.). If you feel uncomfortable using these websites, but so long as you stick to the first page of Google results you should be fine.

The questions you get on these practice tests won't have exactly the same wording as your test, but it'll cover the same material.

Oh, and if you're on the go or prefer a more auditory experience, you might want to check out YouTube. Yes, it's YouTube and you shouldn't believe everything you see on there, but when it comes to CDL Practice tests there's actually a pretty good amount of helpful videos available for free. Most of them are fully voiced too!

Just be sure to check the comments for any redflags or false information. People love to point out stuff like that.

Road Test Prep

We already touched on this before in the introduction but the road test is done no less than 11 days after completing the written test (though you'll probably be scheduling somewhere around a month or three out given availability of testers). You'll need more than two hours to fully accomplish it, and is split into three parts, the pre-inspection test, the driving test, and the post-inspection test, so be sure to use the bathroom beforehand.

Pre-Inspection Prep

How you do your pre-inspection test depends on what kind of vehicle you're driving. The CDL handbook has inspection requirements listed in every chapter and if your state has released its handbook in the current century it should be easy enough to find them on your PDF readers chapter select.

However, no amount of reading will actually prepare you for doing a real inspection. Get a hold of the vehicle you're going to do the test with, the exact vehicle if at all possible, and run through the full inspection with your driving instructor at least once every day you're behind the wheel. Your instructor should already be doing this with you if they are even half-way decent.

The full inspection test should take about an hour, so take your time. It also helps to do your inspections in the same order every time. Just be aware that the person giving you the actual test may try to throw you off by making you do it in the order of their choosing. If they do, don't let them stress you out. Take your time to remember. Most test takers just want to get it over with as much as you do, but they are not allowed to rush you. *You* have the control.

Just remember to always be respectful and pleasant with your test taker. They can, and *will* fail you for mouthing off. I know, it sucks, but they're judging you on your tendency for road rage as well as your knowledge, so think calm thoughts.

Driving Test Prep

Just practice with your driving instructor and do whatever your tester says. I really can't give you much more advice than that.

Post-Inspection Test

It's all the same rules as the pre-inspection. Be respectful, be meticulous, and be chill.

Final Thoughts

And that's it. Hopefully you know more than you did when you started, and maybe had a little chuckle along the way too.

I leave you with this one last piece of advice. When you get nervous, and start stressing out during your test: Think of the chicken nuggets.

Test Taking Strategies and Anxiety Management

Managing Test Anxiety

We have spent a lot of time going over the material you'll find on the test, but let's take one step back and focus on the most important thing in the test-taking process: You.

Getting your CDL is a stressful and expensive process, if you don't think you're going to have at least some anxiety going into this you're kidding yourself. Accepting and managing that anxiety, as well as properly preparing for the test is vital to your success. It doesn't matter how hard or how much you study or how many pretests you ace if your mind goes completely blank at the first question.

The Best Thing You Can Do

First: Seek professional help. I don't mean that as some wisecrack, insult, or sarcasm; I mean find yourself a reliable therapist if you don't have one already. Not only will you drastically increase your chances for passing the CDL, but you'll also just be a generally happier and well-adjusted person.

Now, if you've already got a professional mental health provider, feel free to skip down to Basic Anxiety Management, provided that they are a professional. Friends, family, spouses, and pets that are really good at listening don't count. Having a solid support system is something to be thankful for, but even the best friend in the world isn't going to give you the same help as an accredited therapist.

If you happen to be friends or relatives with a therapist or psychologist, great! Ask them to recommend you to one of their peers because they should know better than to try to treat you themselves.

Common Excuses for Avoiding Care

If you don't have a therapist yet there's probably a reason you've been hesitant about getting one. Let me assure you, if you are a human being then you need to see a mental health professional at least twice a year. Here are some of the more common excuses I get when I ask someone why they aren't.

- "I'm fine! I don't need to see a shrink!"

Okay, first of all, if you're seriously still using outdated lingo like 'shrink' you're probably too old to be trusty behind the wheel of anything more dangerous than a golf cart. Secondly, how do you know you're fine if you haven't at least been to a professional and been evaluated? Your brain is what tells you if something is wrong, so how is it going to tell you if something is wrong with it?

- "I already have a good support system: Family, friends, a volleyball I painted a face on during quarantine, etc."

We already covered this but it must be reiterated. Having a good support system is a great start to looking after your mental health, but it's no substitute for professional therapy and evaluation. Having friends doesn't excuse you from your yearly physical, does it? Why should it excuse you from your bi-yearly mental eval?

Mindfulness and Observation

This one may seem a bit more out there, but many people find it to be the most effective method. The idea behind Mindfulness and Observation Anxiety Management (M.O.A.M.) is to get out of your head by forcing your attention into the present moment. The breakdown looks something like this:

Step 1

Focus your attention on something simple and irrefutable, such as your name and some positive quality about yourself. This can be as simple as "My name is Bob, and I am good at driving." This starting observation should be the same every time; Sort of a designated first step to get you into the proper headspace.

Step 2

Purposefully assess your situation. Make a conscious effort to examine your surroundings. What is something in your immediate vision? What details can you see? Are there any sounds you can identify? How cool is the air around you? The objective here is to slow down your thinking, get out of your head, and re-engage with the present moment.

Step 3

Re-focus on the task at hand. Once you have a calmer and focused mind, turn your attention back to what you were doing.

When to Use It:

Because this method can take quite a bit of time and focus you probably shouldn't try to use it while driving, but it should work fine during a test with no time limit, and any time you pull off to the side of the road following a near-death experience.

Embrace Control

Control is a double-edged sword when it comes to anxiety. Feeling in control does wonders for confidence, but trying too hard to take or maintain that control not only leads to rapidly building anxiety but a whole smorgasbord of other problems. Learning how to let go and be comfortable with things beyond your control is one of the key signs of maturity.

But maturity is going to be one of the last things on your mind when you're having a minor-panic attack while staring at a question you can't answer because your brain is caught in a feedback loop of self-doubt and paranoia. Save the spiritual quest for emotional growth for *after* you get your CDL, and practice these confidence-building habits of control before and during your test.

Control Your Appearance

Pick out the outfit you're going to wear the night before your test. Your clothes are something you always have control over. You don't need to dress up or anything but choose something comfortable that will give you a good confidence boost. Remember that you'll be spending a lot of time sitting down whether you're doing a written or driving test, so skinny jeans and anything that cuts off circulation is probably a bad idea.

Control How You Think

Yes, the entire chapter is basically about how to do this, but the key point here is to not let your mind drift into a negative headspace before the test. If you catch yourself drifting into dark thoughts, clear your head and put it back on track with something positive. Write down a list of positive topics on your phone or a piece of paper, and use it as a prompt. Yes that sounds a bit archaic by today's standards, but social media these days is anything but positive, so use a pre-self-approved list before you go on Twitter to try to calm down.

Control How You Smell

Believe it or not, smell is one of the most powerful senses for emotional control. I shouldn't have to tell you to take a shower and use deodorant before going to take your test, but have you thought about putting on some nice cologne or perfume before heading out? It might not be a bad idea to dab a little something on your collar or wrist. Lavender or citrus blossoms are some of the most common scents used to relax in aromatherapy, but be sure to pick something that works for you.

Smell is also closely tied to memory, so it might not hurt to have that same relaxing smell present while you study.

Pre-Test Emotional Prep

Your best way of keeping anxiety levels down during a test is to start with your anxiety already as low as possible. Here are some final dos and don'ts for managing pre-test jitters.

Do:

- Sleep an appropriate number of hours the night before the test.
- Eat something simple but filling about half an hour before test time. Focus on fresh fruits, proteins, and things easy on your system.
- Take any tests you take one at a time if trying to study for more than one makes you feel overwhelmed. Know your limits, and work comfortably in them.

Don't:

- Stay up all night trying to cram and take a short nap right before the test. It didn't work in high school, it's not going to work now.
- Load up on a carb-heavy meal before your test. You want to be alert, not falling asleep.
- Be rude to the tester or any of the staff. We've gone over this before, but always remember that you can and *will* be failed for bad behavior.
- Take any non-prescription mind-altering substances. We are specifically talking about alcohol and legal marijuana here. Yes, it will help mellow you out, but one of the few requirements for taking the CDL test is sobriety. Prescription anxiety medication is fine, so long as it was prescribed specifically for you by a psychiatrist and you are safe to drive with it.

Finally, if there is one thing you should always do before your test, it's use the bathroom, *especially* before the driving test. It lasts over two hours, and the last thing you want to do is try to parallel park a trailer with a bursting bladder. Take it from me, it's not a fun time.

Bonus Flashcards

Dear future commercial driver, we are grateful for the trust you are giving us by preparing for the CDL Test with our Study Guide. That is why we are happy to share this exclusive and extremely valuable content with you!

Here the 2 main advantages of using our Flashcards:

- Help to store information quickly, facilitating long-term memorization through the "active recall" process, which involves recalling in your mind the same information over and over again. Which is exactly what happens when you train with Flashcards.

- Give you a clear idea of the questions you will be asked in the actual test. This way, your mind will already be used to the test you will face, giving you the right peace of mind to do it without the slightest anxiety. Which often makes the difference between passing or failing.

Are you ready to add this powerful tool to your exam-taking toolbox?
Scan the QR code and get your 200 bonus Flashcards right away:

Dear Future Commercial Driver,

first of all, thank you again for purchasing our product.

Secondly, congratulations! If you are using our Guide, you are among those few who are willing to do whatever it takes to excel on the exam and are not satisfied with just trying.
We create our Study Guides in the same spirit. We want to offer our students only the best to help them get only the best through precise, accurate, and easy-to-use information.

That is why **your success is our success**, and if you think our Guide helped you achieve your goals, we would love it if you could take 60 seconds of your time to leave us a review on Amazon.

Thank you again for trusting us by choosing our Guide, and good luck with your new life as a commercial driver.

Sincerely,

H.S.P. Test Team

Scan the QR code to leave a review (it only takes you 60 seconds):

General Knowledge Test – Questions

1. **During a pre-trip test, what do you check with your instructor during the hose inspection?**

a) Puddles on the ground
b) The dipstick location
c) Frays within the water pump belt
d) The minimum level of windshield water fluid

2. **Which of these scenarios is likely to lead to a vehicle fire?**

a) Spilled fuel cleared swiftly and thoroughly
b) Faulty connections or short circuits
c) Driver smoking within the rest area
d) Combustible cargo with adequate ventilation

3. **Which of the following has a higher likelihood of getting stuck at a railroad crossing that is raised?**

a) Lowboy
b) Car carrier
c) Moving van
d) All of the above

4. **Under which of these two circumstances are you supposed to downshift?**

a) Completing a curve or starting up a hill
b) Completing a curve or starting down a hill
c) Getting into a curve or starting down a hill
d) Getting into a curve or starting up a hill

5. **In which of the following locations do you experience slippery conditions when it's freezing?**

a) A road that looks wet
b) A bridge
c) A shaded place
d) All of the above

6. **In case your vehicle's engine is not overheated, is it a good idea to get off the radiator cap completely?**

a) Yes, provided you have not seen any overflow
b) No
c) Yes, provided your vehicle's radiator is still in good condition
d) Yes

7. **An antilock braking system (ABS)____________________**

a) Ensures your vehicle's wheels do not lock during braking
b) Lessens the braking distance of your vehicle
c) Allows you to drive at a higher speed
d) Enhances the stopping power of the vehicle

8. **While you double your vehicle's speed, by how many times will your vehicle's stopping distance increase?**

a) 3 times more
b) 4 times more
c) 2 times more
d) 5 times more

9. **You intend to turn your vehicle to the right, but you first swing wide to the left. What is likely to happen?**

a) Another driver might attempt to pass you from your right side
b) Your leaf springs might be damaged
c) Another driver might attempt to pass you from the left side
d) All of the above

10. **You are driving a typical tractor-trailer, how long will you take before clearing a double railroad track?**

a) 10 seconds
b) 14 seconds
c) Over 15 seconds
d) Over half an hour

11. **A hazard is________________________**

a) Something that requires a driver to stop
b) Something that a driver can ignore cautiously
c) Something a driver can avoid easily
d) A road condition or user that poses a potential risk

12. Which statement is TRUE about removing air from hot tires?

a) It is not advisable because, upon cooling off, the tires will have a very low pressure
b) It is a brilliant idea to relieve the tires of excess air
c) It does not affect the tires in any way
d) It enables the tires to cool down enabling you to continue your trip thereafter

13. You are driving a 30-foot vehicle at a speed of 55 mph, how many seconds of following distance are you expected to leave?

a) Three seconds
b) Seven seconds
c) Four seconds
d) Six seconds

14. You are approaching a steep downgrade, before you start driving on it, what will determine your speed?

a) The grade's steepness
b) Your vehicle's overall weight, the cargo included
c) The condition of the road
d) All of the above

15. Which of the following critical hand signal can you and your co-driver agree on?

a) "Turn off the music"
b) "Faster"
c) "Go"
d) "Stop"

16. Is it TRUE that the braking system works very well in an empty truck?

a) No
b) Yes
c) Yes; however, this only applies to trucks that were manufactured after 1998
d) Yes; however, it only applies when driving on wet surfaces

17. When you want to begin your trip, how can you ensure you do not roll backward?

a) If necessary, set your parking brake
b) First, engage your clutch and then get the foot off the brake
c) Make use of your trailer's brake hand valve.
d) Take all the above actions

18. Which one of the following is not necessary as part of an emergency kit in your vehicle?

a) A fire extinguisher
b) An extra jacket
c) Warning equipment
d) Spare electrical fuses

19. What is the appropriate action to take when an aggressive driver confronts you?

a) Take your cell phone and contact the police if it can be done safely
b) Resist negative reactions and ignore unpleasant signals
c) Avoid direct eye contact
d) Act in all of the above ways

20. As a commercial driver, you are responsible for all the following EXCEPT?

a) Making sure the sealed cargo is fresh
b) Ensuring the cargo is adequately secured
c) Identifying possible overloads
d) Making sure your cargo is safe

21. How can you best determine the duration of the following distance you have in seconds?

a) Follow the vehicle ahead of you until you are about a quarter closer behind it, then back off once again. Check the time it took you to do this and multiply by four to get the following distance
b) Get your cell phone's stopwatch and use it to find out the duration it takes you to arrive at a mile maker once the vehicle ahead of you has passed it
c) Send your friend a text message and ask him to reply within ten seconds. Find out the distance you have moved within that period
d) Wait for the vehicle ahead of you to pass a landmark or a shadow, and then find out how many seconds it takes you until you reach there

22. Which of the following can help in sobering up a drunk person?

a) A jug of water
b) Time
c) Fresh air
d) Caffeine

23. According to the Commercial Vehicle Safety Alliance (CVSA), roadside inspection should be conducted at eight different levels. Which of the inspection levels is highly comprehensive?

a) Two
b) Five
c) One
d) 8

24. A driver is not permitted to operate a CMV if his/her blood alcohol concentration hits _____ and above.

a) 0.01
b) 0.02
c) 0.06
d) 0.04

25. Except for steering axle tires, the lowest tread depth for any other tire should be ___________inch.

a) 4/32
b) 5/32
c) 2/32
d) 3/32

26. You need a B:C fire extinguisher to put out all the following types of fire EXCEPT?

a) Electrical
b) Gasoline
c) Wood
d) Grease

27. To operate a commercial motor vehicle it is mandatory that you have some specified basic skills. Which one of the following is NOT among the basic skills required?

a) Backing safety
b) Steering
c) Accelerating
d) First aid certification

28. Why is it always advisable that a driver should back toward his/her side?

a) The vehicle will most likely pull toward the side of the driver
b) It makes it easier for the driver to turn the neck
c) The driver can have clear vision, being able to see the rear of the vehicle properly through the side window
d) All the above answers are accurate

29. During wheel bearing seal inspection, what do you check?

a) Twisted axles
b) Leaks
c) Faulty leaf springs
d) Tears

30. During a trip, it is always important to check the following to ensure you're safe on the road, EXCEPT?

a) Mirrors
b) Cargo and their covers
c) Tires
d) Text messages

31. Which of the following answers correctly describes gross vehicle weight (GVW)?

a) The overall weight of one vehicle and its weight included
b) The overall weight of a vehicle, the vehicles being towed, and its load
c) The maximum weight of a single vehicle is indicated by the manufacturing company
d) All of the above

32. When backing you need a helper because_______________________

a) It makes other road users feel more comfortable
b) It is a way of creating a job opportunity for another person
c) There are blind spots
d) All the above reasons

33. Which statement is accurate about retarders?

a) Retarders help a vehicle to slow down, reducing the use of brakes
b) On wet, snowy, or icy roads, retarders should be turned off
c) Your vehicle may encounter skidding if the wheel traction is poor
d) All of the above

34. Which lights should be used more often during night driving?

a) Novelty lights
b) Low beams
c) High beams
d) Four-way flashers

35. What is your responsibility as a commercial driver when transporting sealed cargo?

a) Inspecting a sample of what is contained in the cargo
b) Checking to ensure the axle weight and gross weight limits are not exceeded
c) Checking a picture of what is contained in the cargo to be sure of what you are transporting
d) All of the above

36. If you are found guilty of a second DUI-related offense involving your private vehicle or a CMV, you will be deprived of your CDL driving privileges for_____________

a) Life
b) At least 5 years
c) At least 10 years
d) At least 2 years

37. A vehicle's total stopping distance is equivalent to_____________

a) The sum of braking distance and reaction distance
b) The sum of braking distance, reaction distance, and perception distance
c) The sum of braking distance, viewing distance, and reaction distance
d) The sum of the stopping distance and braking distance

38. During a pre-trip inspection, you are required to keep your starter switch key in the pocket because _____________

a) Another person can steal your truck
b) It can spoil the starting system
c) Another person can start the truck and move it
d) Anything mentioned above can happen

39. Which of the following are you NOT supposed to do when inspecting the cab and starting the engine?

a) Start the engine, and then try to get any unusual sounds
b) Examine the air pressure gauge
c) Examine the transmission controls
d) First, start the engine, and then place the gearshift in neutral

40. What is the best thing to do in an accident scene to make sure it does not lead to other accidents?

a) Take a drink to help you relax your nerves.
b) Do not step out of your vehicle up to the moment help arrives
c) Place a warning sign to ensure other drivers do not run into the scene
d) Come out of the vehicle, take no action, and move to a raised ground

41. Which of these parts constitutes the primary component of steering?

a) Gearbox
b) Torque rod
c) Leaf spring
d) Bearing plate

42. Which of the following statements best describes hazardous materials placards?

a) They are signs that cautions people to keep at least 1000 feet away from vehicles
b) They are signs that tax collectors use to calculate the amount of tax hazardous cargo should fetch
c) They are signs placed outside a vehicle to indicate its cargo's hazardous class.
d) They are signs placed on the interior of a vehicle to remind the driver what the vehicle is transporting

43. A 20-foot load should have ___________tiedowns.

a) Three
b) Four
c) One
d) Two

44. How do you know whether your vehicle is fitted with the ABS (antilock braking system)?

a) The trailer has a yellow ABS malfunction lamp on its left side, either on the rear or front corner
b) If it has a yellow ABS malfunction light on its instrument panel.
c) If it has wheel speed sensor cables originating from its rear brakes
d) All of the above

45. By what fraction should you reduce your speed when driving on a wet road?

a) ¼
b) ½
c) 1/3
d) 60%

46. Whenever you are on a trip, you must have _________reflective warning triangles in your vehicle for emergencies.

a) 1
b) 2
c) 4
d) 3

47. What speed over the posted speed limit is regarded as excessive speeding?

a) 3 mph
b) 10 mph
c) 15 mph
d) 5 mph

48. What happens to the anti-lock braking system indicator lights when the ABS is in operation?

a) They stay on
b) They light up and go off
c) They blink hazardously
d) They do not behave in any of the above manners

49. A CDL driver should look ____________seconds ahead while driving?

a) 9 to 12
b) 12 to 15
c) 3 to 7
d) 18 to 20

50. Which of the following is the correct meaning of tire load index?

a) Specifications of what the tire is made of
b) The amount of weight a vehicle's tire can carry safely at a certain pressure
c) The overall weight of a tire
d) The quality rating of a tire

General Knowledge Test – Answers

1. **Answer: a).** During hose inspection, when doing your pre-trip test, you are required to check for any leaks, like puddles on the ground and fluids that might be dipping beneath the transmission or engine. The hoses are also examined for other issues, such as cracks.
2. **Answer: b).** Spilled fuel, combustible cargo, and smoking have potential risks. However, when correctly managed they shouldn't trigger fire unless under exclusive circumstances like faulty connections and short circuits.
3. **Answer: d).** Low combination vehicles that are likely to get stuck at a high railroad crossing are the low-slung units such as moving vans, lowboys, carrier cars, etc. The other type includes single-axle tractors tied to a long trailer with the landing gear designed to work with a tandem-axle tractor. You need to be very cautious when driving this kind of vehicle across railroad crossings.
4. **Answer: c).** It is important to downshift before you start a hill since it allows you to make good use of your engine braking. It is advisable that you downshift to the required gear – a gear is usually below the one needed to drive uphill. When you downshift before a curve, you enhance the vehicle's stability and enable the vehicle to acquire the power needed to accelerate off the turn.
5. **Answer: d).** when the temperature reaches the freezing point, particular road sections begin to freeze followed by others. The shaded places and bridges are usually the first ones to freeze. A road that looks wet sometimes is covered with a thin layer of black ice that is slippery and transparent through which the road is visible.
6. **Answer: b).** It is not sufficient for your vehicle's engine not to overheat. You must wait for the cooling system to completely cool before trying to get off the radiator cap. As you do that, you need to exercise a lot of caution since you might still encounter hazardous fluids and steam, as well as tremendous pressure.
7. **Answer: a).** ABS only comes into play to ensure your vehicle's wheels do not lock, which can result in skidding. It is not the function of ABS to alter how you brake during other times. You should therefore not use it as an alternative for careful braking, regular maintenance, proper brakes, or defensive driving.
8. **Answer: b).** When your vehicle's speed doubles, the distance that the vehicle takes before it can stop also increases by about the square of the speed increases – to almost 4 times more than the initial speed. For instance, when you increase the speed from 15 to 30 mph, your vehicle's stopping distance will rise from 46 feet to 148 feet.
9. **Answer a).** Swinging wide to the left when you intend to turn right is usually not a good idea because another driver might think you want to change lanes and be tempted to pass your vehicle on the right. Rather, use your vehicle's rear to make a right turn and ensure you are closer to the curb and then turn wide as you finish your turn. If you do this, there will be no space on the right for a driver to pass.
10. **Answer: c).** when operating a typical-tractor trailer, expect to spend over 15 seconds clearing a double track and a minimum of 14 seconds when clearing a single track.
11. **Answer: d).** A hazard refers to a road condition or user that poses a potential risk. It is something that can cause a disaster but can be avoided if the driver is cautious or vigilant.
12. **Answer: a).** When your vehicle's tires become hot, it increases the air pressure. But letting out excess pressure from the tires will leave them with insufficient pressure when they cool again, and that may cause them to blow out or catch fire. When your tires become so hot that you cannot handle them, stop and give them time to cool down.
13. **Answer: c).** To determine the following distance, you use the one second per ten feet of vehicle formula, and an additional second in case you are driving at a speed of more than 40 mph. So, if you are driving a 30-feet vehicle at a speed of 55 mph, you need to leave 4 seconds following distance.
14. **Answer: d).** When you want to drive down a steep downgrade, you first need to decide the speed you

will use. The speed you choose should be influenced by the steepness of the downgrade, the length, your vehicle's overall weight including the cargo, the condition of the road as well as weather.

15. **Answer: d).** When an accident occurs, there is no way it can be reversed. This explains why it is highly important for you and your helper to come up with a straightforward hand signal for "Stop." With that, you can immediately stop whatever activity you're involved in to curb an accident.

16. **Answer: a).** Brakes work well in trucks when the trucks are utilized according to their design: carrying well-balanced cargo. When a truck is loaded properly, braking works well because of the increased traction and this reduces the stopping distance. On the other hand, empty trucks normally have a longer stopping distance due to less traction.

17. **Answer: d).** In case you are operating a vehicle with a manual transmission, partially engage, and then remove your right foot from the brake. If necessary, set your vehicle's parking brake to prevent it from rolling back. Only release your parking brake after applying sufficient engine power to avoid rolling back. If it's a tractor-trailer fitted with a trailer brake hand valve, you can make use of the hand valve to ensure it does not roll back.

18. **Answer: b).** Even though you need a jacket especially when the weather is cold, it doesn't fall on the list of emergency kits. In your vehicle, there must be some spare electrical fuses (except for vehicles fitted with circuit breakers), warning equipment such as reflective triangles and flares, and a properly functioning fire extinguisher.

19. **Answer: d).** When you face a confrontation from an aggressive driver, avoid giving the person a confrontation in return. Rather, reach out to the police via your phone if you're in a position to do that safely, look for peace by not reacting negatively to unpleasant signals, and ignore the person by not keeping eye contact.

20. **Answer: a).** As a cargo transporter, it is not your duty to check the freshness of sealed cargo, nor are you supposed to inspect it. Your responsibilities only include checking the safety of your load and making sure it is well-balanced, not overloaded, and secured.

21. **Answer: d).** Calculate the time your vehicle takes to arrive at a specific stationary object once the vehicle in front passes it. You can count your seconds this way: 1001, 1002 ..." The alternative approaches in the remaining options are either ineffective or dangerously distracting. Keep in mind that you must increase your following distance in situations where there is heavy traffic, the presence of heavy vehicles, higher speeds, or poor weather.

22. **Answer: b).** When you take alcohol; the body breaks it down at a rate that is predictable. This is usually one standard drink for every hour, and one standard drink is equivalent to a single 12-ounce bottle of beer, 5 ounces of wine, and 1.5 ounces of hard brew. Not even fresh air, water, or coffee can raise that rate. So, the best remedy is to give the alcohol time to break down.

23. **Answer: c).** The Commercial Vehicle Safety Alliance (CVSA) came up with the National Roadside Inspection Program. According to the program, there are 8 stages of inspections, and every one of them focuses on specific items. In the first level, a comprehensive inspection is conducted- it checks both the vehicle and the driver. The inspecting officer examines the vehicle by practically getting under the vehicle and walking around it to check whether any defects can be detected. The second level's activities are almost of the same magnitude as level 1, except that the inspector does not enter underneath your vehicle. It only involves a walkaround.

24. **Answer: d).** As a CMV driver, you face the risk of losing your CDL for a minimum of one year in case you are found guilty of operating a CMV with a 0.04 or more BAC.

25. **Answer: c).** Only steering axle tires are required to have a minimum tread depth of 4/32 inch. The rest of the tires should not have anything less than 2/32 inch.

26. **Answer: c).** B:C fire extinguishers are used to put out fires that you cannot extinguish using ordinary water. These may include fires caused by grease, gasoline, and electricity. However, ordinary combustible materials such as wood, cloth, paper, etc. do not necessarily need a B:C fire

extinguisher since they can be put out using water or an extinguisher with an A rating.

27. **Answer: d).** There are four basic skills you need before you can qualify to operate as a commercial driver. These are backing safely, stopping, steering, and accelerating. Even though being a certified first aider might be helpful at certain times in your profession, it doesn't fall under the basic skills.

28. **Answer: c).** Drivers are always required to back toward their side since it makes it easier to see objects. For instance, it is easier to check the rear of the vehicle through the side window. In case the truck pulls in whichever direction, it should be serviced. The comfort of the neck should not compromise a driver's safety.

29. **Answer: b).** The most probable problem you can encounter in wheel bearing seals is leakages. Therefore, it is important to check for any signs of leaks or cracks and even grease.

30. **Answer: d).** While in transit, it is always important to monitor all critical components of your vehicle including mirrors, tires, gauges, cargo, and other instruments. Your cell phone should always be kept away throughout the trip.

31. **Answer: a).** Gross Vehicle Weight (GVW) refers to the weight of only one vehicle with its load included.

32. **Answer: c).** The services of a helper are highly needed during backing since you will be encountering blind spots that you are unable to see. When starting, you and your helper should settle on hand signals for "Stop" (very important) and "Go".

33. **Answer: d).** Whilst retarders are important in reducing overreliance on braking, in cases where your vehicle has poor wheel traction or during inclement weather, they can cause the wheels to skid. So, you should make sure your retarders are off during poor weather.

34. **Answer: c).** Driving at night requires you to utilize the high beams if you want to see further provided it is permitted and safe and that it will not interfere with the vision of other drivers. The headlight lights also should be dimmed anytime you are 500 feet near an oncoming vehicle or 500 feet behind a vehicle.

35. **Answer: b).** Even though you are not permitted to inspect cargo that is sealed, you still have the responsibility to make sure the cargo you are transporting does not surpass the gross and axle weight limits. Therefore, it's very important to ascertain that.

36. **Answer a).** Upon a second conviction based on another DUI offense, your CDL privileges will be revoked for life. A 0.04% BAC or more is regarded as DUI when driving a CMV. The first offense gets you a warning and offers you an opportunity to look for a remedy, however, the second offense deprives you of your job.

37. **Answer: b).** The total stopping distance of a vehicle is equivalent to the sum of braking distance (the distance a vehicle continues to move after applying the brake) + reaction distance (the distance a vehicle moves from the moment the brain triggers your foot to act to the time the foot begins to brake) + perception distance (the distance your vehicle moves from the moment you spot a hazard to the time the brain process it).

38. **Answer: c).** During your pre-trip inspection session, you would not wish anybody (for example your co-driver) who is not aware of where you are to start the vehicle and place your life in danger.

39. **Answer: d).** Remember the question is asking which one are you "NOT". When conducting this part of the inspection, you are supposed to first put your gearshift in neutral, and then start the engine. When the engine is on, pay attention to any unusual sounds. After checking the engine, now examine the controls and gauges, including transmission controls and air pressure gauges.

40. **Answer: c).** If you have not been injured, you are responsible to make sure that other drivers can see your vehicles that have been involved in the accident and avoid bumping into them. Put the warning devices as soon as possible to prevent further accidents like pile-ups.

41. **Answer: a).** The gearbox is the most critical component of a steering system. The torque rod, leaf spring, and bearing plate form part of the suspension system.

42. **Answer c).** Hazardous materials placards refer to a set of four regulated signs that are usually

displayed on the outside of a vehicle to indicate the hazard class of cargo to ensure who are interested to know such as the cargo handlers or emergency service staff are aware of it.

43. **Answer: d).** According to the rule, every ten feet of cargo requires one tiedown, and each load notwithstanding the length should have a minimum of two tie-downs. Therefore, if a cargo is 20 feet, it needs two tie-downs.

44. **Answer: d).** Most of the modern vehicles fitted with ABS also have a light installed on their instrument panel which switches on briefly any time the vehicle starts to remind the driver about the ABS. Trailers are fitted with yellow ABS malfunction lamps which can be found on the left rear corner or left front corner. Also, you can check if your vehicle has cables originating from the brakes.

45. **Answer: c).** On a wet road, your vehicle's stopping speed increases, so you need to reduce the speed by a third. When driving on snow, reduce the speed by half the normal speed. Driving on icy roads requires you to slow to a crawl, then stop the vehicle as soon as that can be done safely.

46. **Answer d).** The following must be included in the emergency equipment of your truck; warning devices including fuses, liquid burning flares, and reflective red triangles. Fuses are usually 6, red reflective triangles 3, and liquid burning flares 3.

47. **Answer: c).** If you drive at a speed that is 15 mph more than the posted speed limit, then you'll be considered to be driving at an excessive speed.

48. **Answer: b).** With an ABS that is functioning, the anti-lock braking system indicator lights switch on and then go off.

49. **Answer: b).** Drivers of commercial vehicles are required to look 12 to 15 seconds ahead while driving. This is because changing lanes or stopping requires lots of distance. Looking properly ahead helps the driver to make safe moves in case anything happens.

50. **Answer: b).** Tire load index refers to the total weight a tire can safely carry at a given pressure. For instance, a tire with a load index of 92, can carry a load of about 1,389 pounds with maximum air pressure.

Air Brakes Test – Questions

1. The front wheel brakes work best under which conditions?

a) All weather conditions
b) Only icy or wet conditions
c) Only good weather
d) None of the above conditions

2. You should utilize the parking brake__________________

a) Whenever you leave the vehicle, with some exceptions
b) Only when in urban areas where vehicles are many
c) Whenever you leave the vehicle regardless of the time you will be out
d) Only if you leave the vehicle for an extended time length

3. Which of the following is the correct procedure to follow when testing the low air pressure warning signal of a vehicle?

a) Manually release air from the brakes and check whether the signal comes on
b) Pump your brakes as the engine runs
c) Pump your brakes until you achieve a below 30 psi air pressure
d) Ensure the engine is off, and then step on and off your brake pedal to achieve a below 55 psi air pressure

4. Which of these parts does NOT belong to the air brake system?

a) Parking brake system
b) Radio signal system
c) Service brake system
d) Emergency brake system

5. Which statement is TRUE about slack adjusters?

a) They are located between the push rod on the disc brakes and the power screw
b) They are a component of the air brake system used in adjusting the brakes
c) They are located between S-cam on the drum brakes and the push rod
d) All of the above is true

6. Which of the following shows the correct way of checking the slack adjusters of your vehicle?

a) Press your brake pedal as you listen to any strange sound
b) Using gloves pull any reachable slack adjuster hard
c) Accelerate and brake hard
d) All of the above

7. What is the main role of an anti-braking system (ABS)?

a) It shortens the stopping distance of a vehicle
b) It increases a vehicle's normal braking capacity
c) It decreases a vehicle's normal braking capacity
d) It activates to prevent the wheels from locking up

8. What is common about vehicles that have air brakes?

a) They all have an air use gauge
b) They all have a backup hydraulic system
c) They all have a supply pressure gauge
d) None of the above

9. What is the maximum acceptable leakage rate per minute after the initial pressure drop when testing air leakage rate?

a) 6 psi if it's a combination vehicle and 5 psi if it's a single vehicle
b) 4 psi if it's a combination vehicle and 3 psi if it's a single vehicle
c) 3 psi if it's a combination vehicle and 1 psi if it's a single vehicle
d) 10 psi if it's a combination vehicle and 5 psi if it's a single vehicle

10. A supply pressure gauge____________________

a) Warns you only when your tank has insufficient air
b) Indicates the amount of air pressure available in the tank
c) Tells you the level of hotness of the air available in the tan
d) Tells you all of the above

11. The pressure available in your vehicle's air tank must fall below________psi before a low air pressure warning signal can come on.

a) 60-55
b) 70-75
c) 80-85
d) 90-95

12. The following are components of a drum brake. Which one is NOT?

a) Safety valve
b) Return spring
c) Slack adjuster
d) Brake drum

13. Which statement is TRUE about a tractor protection valve?

a) It automatically closes when your air supply reduces to a particular level
b) It provides your brake system with air supply
c) It closes when parking brakes are applied.
d) It does all of the above

14. The safety valve normally opens at ______psi.

a) 250
b) 100
c) 150
d) 200

15. Brake fail or brake fade is caused by ________________________.

a) Failure to adequately rely on engine braking
b) Brakes that are out of adjustment
c) Overusing the service brakes
d) All of the above

16. Which vehicles are required to have low air pressure warning signals?

a) All vehicles manufactured after 2005
b) None; it is optional
c) Vehicles manufactured after 2010
d) All vehicles that are currently in use and have air-pressure brakes

17. Failure to drain air tanks_________________.

a) This may lead to brake failure due to the freezing of water
b) May increase the speed at which you drive.
c) Will make your side brake fail
d) This may lead to the draining out of transmission fluid

18. What is the right time to drain your vehicle's air tanks?

a) Whenever you reach the end of your working day
b) When you reach the end of your fiscal quarter
c) Whenever you end a trip
d) End of every month

19. When driving downhill, you only use air brakes to supplement___________.

a) The limiting valve of your front brakes
b) The engine's braking effect
c) The spring brake usage
d) None of the above

20. Whenever you leave your vehicle unattended, you should_____________.

a) Carry the keys along
b) Chock your wheels
c) Apply your parking brakes
d) Do all the above

21. What is the impact of faulty ABS on the functioning of your truck's brakes?

a) Your truck will slow to a halt and you will be forced to pull over
b) It causes problems to other mechanical systems which can lead to a fire
c) Your brakes will still work as usual but you will have to ensure the ABS is fixed soon
d) Your brake function will completely be ineffective causing the truck to be out of control

22. Which statement is TRUE about spring brakes?

a) They become effective when the psi falls to a particular range, usually between 20 and 30 PSI
b) They are brakes that automatically come on a tractor or truck when the PSI falls too low
c) They consist of powerful springs that switch on the brakes when air pressure is lost
d) All of the above

23. What can you do to dry out wet brakes?

a) Utilize the brakes as you drive in low gear
b) You must take them to the mechanic for service
c) Use them to slow down
d) Drain your air storage tanks

24. You should avoid ______________________ when your spring brakes are on.

a) Pushing down your brake pedal
b) Pressing down your gas pedal
c) Utilizing your modulating valve
d) Checking the level of air in your air tanks

25. What causes the air brakes to delay a bit when stopping?

a) The time needed for the flow of air from the lines to the brakes
b) The time needed for building up sufficient pressure for brakes engagement
c) The time needed for the compressed air to engage the push rod
d) The time needed for the air brake system to determine the right pressure quantity to relay to each wheel

Air Brakes Test – Answers

1. **Answer: a).** Front wheel brakes operate well under any weather as well as driving conditions. You are not likely to experience a skid with the front when braking even on icy roads.

2. **Answer: a).** You should use the parking brakes any time you leave the vehicle regardless of the length of time you will be out. The only time you might not do so is when the brakes are very hot or wet and there is a high likelihood of them freezing.

3. **Answer: d).** When testing the low air pressure warning signal of your vehicle, the best procedure to apply is to first release your parking brake (any kind of vehicle), release the tractor protection valve (for combination vehicles), and then turn the engine off the vehicle and leave the electrical power on. Finally, step on the brake pedal and then off. Upon hitting a pressure of below 55 psi, the low air pressure warning signal needs to come on. You don't need to go down to 30 psi.

4. **Answer: b).** The air brakes consist of three systems: the emergency brake, the parking brake, and the service brake.

5. **Answer: d).** Slack adjusters form an important component of the air brake system that makes it easier to adjust your brakes making sure they remain safe. They can be found in different locations, depending on the kind of brakes in your vehicle.

6. **Answer: b).** When checking the slack adjusters, wear your gloves and try pulling on them manually. In case you realize an inch or additional "give," then there is a problem that needs to be fixed.

7. **Answer: d).** ABS doesn't play a great role in your usual driving. It neither impacts the braking capability of your vehicle nor shortens its stopping distance. It does ensure you have control while driving by activating whenever the wheels want to lock up.

8. **Answer: c).** All vehicles fitted with air brakes also have a supply pressure gauge. The supply pressure gauge indicates the amount of air pressure present for braking.

9. **Answer: b).** The maximum acceptable leakage in every minute following the initial pressure drop when testing air leakage rate is 4 psi if it's a combination vehicle and 3 psi if it's a single vehicle. In case of a higher leakage rate, any possibilities of leaks should be checked and fixed. Air leakage test is usually done as part of air brake systems inspection.

10. **Answer: b).** The work of a supply pressure gauge is to show you of the amount of air available in the tank at any time. Some vehicles have their supply pressure gauges connected to warning lights or bells.

11. **Answer: a).** Your vehicle's low air pressure warning light or bell has to come on whenever the air pressure is less than 60-55 psi. The warning light may come on at a bit higher pressure in particular vehicles. Refer to the specifications of the manufacturer.

12. **Answer: a).** Each axle in a vehicle has drum brakes and it consists of about 10 different parts, such as the brake drum, slack adjuster, and return spring. Even though the safety valve falls under the components of the air brake system, it is not one of the drum brake parts.

13. **Answer: d).** The tractor protection valve guards the airbrake system by closing when the parking brakes are applied, automatically closing when your supply falls to a very low level and providing the air brake with air supply.

14. **Answer: c).** The safety valve, whose function is to guard the system against excessive pressure, is normally set so that it can open whenever the system hits 150 psi.

15. **Answer: d).** Brake fail and brake fade are usually a result of using brakes in an incorrect way leading to excess heat. Usually, this is due to overusing the service brakes, failure to adequately rely on engine brakes, poor adjustment of brakes, as well as any other mechanical reason, and human error.

16. **Answer: d).** Any vehicle operating today that has air brakes is required to have a low air pressure warning signal.

17. **Answer: a).** Air tanks contain a mix of compressor oil and water. When the mixture is left to accumulate at the bottom, the water is likely to freeze, and when that happens, your brakes may fail.

18. **Answer: a).** If you do not have a vehicle that drains its air tanks automatically, you need to make sure you drain the tanks whenever you reach the end of your working day to prevent the oil and moisture from coagulating or freezing which may lead to brake failure.

19. **Answer: b).** When driving downhill, make sure your engine is in a low gear to maintain a low speed, and utilize your air brakes as a supplement to slow down.

20. **Answer: d).** Anytime you leave your vehicle unattended, you should set your parking brakes and chock your wheels. Getting the keys off your vehicle is a basic safety measure for all kinds of vehicles including passenger vehicles.

21. **Answer: c).** A faulty ABS will not influence any basic component of your truck, the brakes will function as usual. Just use the brakes and make sure the ABS is fixed soon. You don't have to be worried unless there is a serious warning from your system.

22. **Answer: d).** Spring brakes are brakes that become effective whenever the psi goes down to a particular range, in most cases 20 to 30 PSI. They also start functioning automatically whenever PSI levels are too low, however, in normal circumstances you need to ensure your vehicle doesn't reach this level. Finally, spring brakes consist of powerful springs that ensure your brakes come on when they detect a loss in air pressure due to some factors such as a leak.

23. **Answer: a).** When your brakes are wet, you can apply them as you drive in low gear. Through this, the brakes will heat up and dry.

24. **Answer: a).** You should never push your brake pedal when your spring brakes are on because the combination of air pressure and springs can damage your brakes.

25. **Answer: a).** As opposed to hydraulic brakes which work instantly, air brakes have a delay of about 0.5 seconds which is the time needed for the air to flow to the brakes through the lines before the brakes start to function.

Double/Triple Test – Questions

1. **You want to apply emergency braking to avoid a crash while driving with double trailers. You can achieve this by_________________.**

a) Applying the trailer brakes
b) Stepping on the brake pedal very hard without getting your removing your leg
c) Applying stab or controlled braking

2. **When pulling multiple trailers, the ________trailer should come just behind your tractor.**

a) Lightest
b) Heaviest
c) Shortest

3. **If you unlock the pintle hook when the dolly is still underneath the second trailer____________.**

a) The dolly's tow bar is likely to fly up
b) The air lines are likely to rapture
c) Nothing is likely to happen unless your rig rolls forward

4. **The following statements refer to checking your mirrors. Which one is TRUE?**

a) Mirrors should be used to keep an eye on the tires
b) Mirrors can be accurately adjusted while driving in traffic
c) If properly adjusted, mirrors can get rid of blind spots

5. **A converter dolly is made up of a _____wheel and ___________axles.**

a) Fifth; 2 or 3
b) Third; 2 or 3
c) Fifth; 1 or 2

6. **Which of the following statements correctly describes a converter dolly?**

a) An electronic device used in international trucking to convert electricity between a semitrailer and a tractor-trailer
b) An electronic device used to connect electricity to the tractor-trailer's rear from a semitrailer
c) A device used during coupling to connect a semitrailer to the tractor-trailer's rear

7. **When uncoupling a converter dolly you should start by_______________**

a) Lowering its landing gear
b) Gently clearing of it
c) Disconnecting its safety chains

8. **You are driving a double-trailer combination of 100-foot length at a speed of 50 mph on a dry road with good visibility. What is the minimum distance you should keep ahead of you in seconds?**

a) 11 seconds
b) 10 seconds
c) 9 seconds

9. **Which of the following statements is TRUE about empty trucks?**

a) An empty truck can stop easily because no cargo will shift
b) Empty trucks may experience poor traction because of wheel lockup and bouncing
c) Empty trucks have reduced stopping distance compared to loaded trucks

10. **How can you position your converter dolly over a short distance?**

a) You can move it by hand
b) You can ask for help from your dispatcher
c) You can assign the shipper to do it

11. Which statement is TRUE about managing spaces to the sides?

a) While on multilane roads avoid driving alongside other vehicles
b) Always drive to the right of your lane
c) High winds do not have any impact on doubles and triples

12. When conducting a walk-around inspection of your power-operated landing gear, what should you check for?

a) Hydraulic fluid or air leaks
b) Grime or dirt
c) Gasoline or water leaks

13. A converter dolly equipped with antilock brakes (ABS) has ________________________.

a) A red lamp on the right side
b) A yellow lamp on the right side
c) A yellow lamp on the left side

14. If you have to drive through flowing water or deep puddles, you can do all the following EXCEPT?

a) Driving through quickly
b) Engaging a lower gear
c) Increasing engine RPM

15. You want to park your double/triple combination. What type of parking space should you look for?

a) A parking space where you can back out of
b) A parking space that is closer to your destination
c) A parking space where you can drive straight through

16. What do you check during the visual inspection of coupling?

a) That there is no space between the fifth wheel and the trailer apron. Closed locking jaws on the kingpin
b) That there is adequate space between the fifth wheel and the trailer apron
c) That there is adequate grease on the fifth wheel

17. How should you release the dolly brakes while coupling twin trailers?

a) Drop your trailer onto the fifth wheel
b) Release the air from the brake line
c) Open the air tank petcock

18. Where should you park the rig while uncoupling your double trailers?

a) On a soft surface
b) On level ground
c) In the parking lot of your company

19. Where will you find cut-out cocks (shut-off valves) on trailers that serve as doubles and triples?

a) Only on the parking brake system
b) On the emergency and service brakes air lines
c) On the emergency air lines

20. Which of the following statements about the shut-off valves is TRUE?

a) The shut-off valves (cut-out cocks) on the rearmost trailer should be closed
b) All shut-off valves (cut-out cocks) need to be open
c) The rearmost trailer doesn't have shut-off valves (cut-out cocks)

Double/Triple Test – Answers

1. **Answer: c).** If you apply hard brakes and turn at the same time, you are likely to experience a skid. Therefore, you need to apply your brakes in a manner that will ensure your vehicle maintains a straight line and gives you room to turn when necessary. If you want to apply an emergency brake to avoid crashing, use stab or controlled braking if your vehicle is equipped with ABS.

2. **Answer: b).** The chances of the rearmost trailer rolling over are higher compared to the front trailer. You should place the heaviest trailer just behind your tractor and put the lightest trailer last.

3. **Answer: a).** Unlocking the pintle hook when the dolly is still underneath your rear trailer may cause the dolly's tow bar to fly up. When this happens, it might be difficult to recouple, and may cause injuries.

4. **Answer: a).** Mirrors should be cleaned and adjusted during your pre-trip inspection, while the vehicle is parked. Adjust the mirrors to ensure you can have a view of part of the roadway and your vehicle. The mirrors can only be accurately adjusted when the trailers are straight. While on the road, you should be able to keep an eye on the tires through your mirrors. This is one of the ways to notice a tire fire. Note that blind spots will continue to be out of view no matter how carefully you adjust the mirrors.

5. **Answer: c).** Just like a typical rear of a tractor, a converter dolly has a fifth wheel as well as 1 or 2 axles, so a semitrailer can be connected to it.

6. **Answer: c).** The main role of a converter dolly is to link a semitrailer and the rear of a tractor-trailer to form a triple or double combination. The dolly comes between the semitrailer and the tractor-trailer.

7. **Answer: a).** When uncoupling the converter dolly, the first step involves lowering the dolly landing gear. Once this is done, the safety chains are disconnected, and the chock wheels or converter gear spring brakes are applied, release the pintle hook on the first semi-trailer, and finally slowly pull off the dolly.

8. **Answer: a).** To determine the following distance, keep in mind that every ten feet of a vehicle is given one second, and if driving at a speed more than 40 mph, an extra second is added. So, for a vehicle of length 100 feet driving at a speed of 50 mph, you will determine the following distance by dividing 100 by 10, and then because the speed is over 40 mph, add one (100/10+1 =11).

9. **Answer: b).** Trucks' brakes function best when they do what they are designed to carry a load that is properly balanced. Unloaded trucks have less traction than loaded trucks, resulting in a longer stopping distance.

10. **Answer: a).** For shorter distances, you can move your dolly by hand to put it in line with your kingpin.

11. **Answer: a).** When driving on multilane roads, you should try as much as possible not to drive directly alongside another vehicle. The driver of the other vehicle might fail to see you, and his or her vehicle may bump into yours when changing lanes. Always try to drop back or move ahead when driving in the blind spot of another vehicle.

12. **Answer: a).** During a walk-around inspection of your power-operated landing gear, you should ensure there is no hydraulic fluid or air leak. In case you encounter any leakages, these must be fixed immediately.

13. **Answer: c).** Converter dollies made after March 1, 1998, are fitted with antilock brakes. These converter dollies have a yellow lamp on their left side.

14. **Answer: a).** You should try as much as possible not to drive through deep-flowing water or puddles. However, if you must, make sure you slow down and that your transmission is on low gear. Put on your brakes gently. Increase your engine rpm and keep light pressure on your brakes as you cross the water.

15. **Answer: c).** When looking for a space to park your double or triple combination, you should make sure it is a spot where you can drive straight through. Avoid any parking spot that will require

you to back out because when backing, you are not able to see everything behind you, which makes it more dangerous.

16. **Answer: a).** When performing your visual check of coupling, make sure there is no space between the fifth wheel plate and your trailer apron, and that your locking jaws are closed on the kingpin.
17. **Answer: c).** To release the dolly brakes, you should open your air tank valve (petcock), or if it's a dolly with spring brakes, you can utilize the parking brake control.
18. **Answer: b).** When uncoupling your double trailers, you should park the vehicle in a straight line on firm, level ground and apply the parking brakes to make sure your vehicle doesn't move.
19. **Answer: b).** Trailers that are used as doubles and triples have shut-off valves for both the emergency and service air lines.
20. **Answer: a).** You should make sure the shut-off valves (cut-out cocks) on the rear of your last trailer are closed

Hazardous Materials (HAZMAT) Test – Questions

1. **Which of these materials can you use as floor liners when transporting materials classified as Division 1.1 or 1.2?**

a) Non-ferrous metal
b) Stainless steel
c) Carbon steel
d) All of the above materials

2. **What is the responsibility of shippers during the packing of material?**

a) Ensure the packages can be opened and closed easily
b) Ensure the package is light
c) Ensure the package can be identified easily
d) Ensure all of the above

3. **What is the best action to take when you discover leakage in the shipment of hazardous materials at a rest stop and you don't have any phone around?**

a) Continue driving at a lower speed and carefully until you reach a place you can get a phone
b) Get someone to send for help and give the person all the necessary details
c) Continue driving quickly until you reach where you can get help
d) Park the truck and ensure the emergency lights are on, and then walk for help

4. **You've already loaded your truck with silver cyanide weighing 100 pounds, what action should you take if you are given documentation at a dock that requires you to add 100 cartons of battery acid to your cargo?**

a) Refuse to load the battery acid
b) Ensure the battery acid is loaded on the silver cyanide
c) Ensure the silver cyanide is loaded on the battery acid
d) Ensure there is adequate space between the battery acid and silver cyanide

5. **In which two places will you find the hazardous materials identification number?**

a) On the packages and shipping paperwork at the origin
b) On the shipping paperwork as well as packages
c) On the shipping paperwork at the destination as well as the packages
d) On a secret documentation in the driver's wallet and on the shipping paperwork

6. **How far should placards be placed from the rest of the markings?**

a) 8 inches
b) 3 inches
c) 12 inches
d) 12 inches

7. **Apart from the packaging and shipping papers, which other two locations must the hazardous material identification number be displayed?**

a) On a sticker within the glove compartment
b) On a sticker within the glove compartment and the gas tank
c) On your steering wheel and on an interim license plate holder
d) On the cargo tanks and all the bulk packages

8. **In addition to information describing hazardous materials, which other information should be contained in Hazmat shipping paperwork?**

a) Information concerning emergency response
b) The driver's next of kin's contact details
c) Their monetary value
d) All of the above information

9. Which of the following information correctly describes a "safe haven"?

a) It is a location where you can park unattended vehicles transporting explosives
b) It is a slang term used to refer to the location where you park your vehicle carrying hazardous materials when you reach the end of your driving day.
c) It is a place where you can safely dispose of hazardous materials
d) It is a location where you stay after reporting your employer for illegal dealings

10. Drivers should placard their vehicles because______________

a) It cautions people with children to use another lane
b) It provides drivers with something interesting to look at as they drive
c) It forces other drivers to keep a 20-foot distance in any direction
d) It helps communicate risk

11. If you are driving a placarded vehicle, how far from the nearest railroad crossing or bridge must you stop?

a) 10 to 35 feet
b) 15-50 feet
c) 5-20 feet
d) None of the above

12. What must be done on the shipping paper for a shipment containing both non-hazardous and hazardous materials?

a) The hazardous materials have to come first on the list
b) The hazardous materials should be highlighted using a different color
c) Any of the above
d) None of the above

13. What is the minimum of a fire extinguisher that placarded vehicles can carry?

a) 5 A:B
b) 10 B:C
c) 5 B:C
d) 10 A:B

14. What are the key features that make portable tanks different from cargo tanks?

a) Filling of portable tanks is done off the vehicle; filling of cargo tanks is done on the vehicle
b) Portable tanks are not required to have the lessee's or owner's name displayed; cargo tanks are required to have the lessee's or owner's name displayed on them
c) Portable tanks are attached temporarily; cargo tanks are permanently attached to the vehicle
d) All of the above key differences

15. The following statements refer to the Emergency Guidebook (ERG), which one is TRUE?

a) It was prepared by the United States Department of Transportation and is used across the nation
b) The emergency personnel study it to help them assure the public of their safety
c) It contains a hazardous materials identification number index (which is why correct labeling of things is needed)
d) All the above statements are true

16. Should you stop as you approach a railroad crossing while hauling Division 4.3 materials weighing 100 pounds?

a) Yes; however, if only there is an arm down signaling vehicles to stop
b) You cannot tell unless you have additional information
c) Yes
d) No

17. Which of the following factors cannot help you decide which placards to display on your vehicle?

a) The quantity of all the hazardous materials belonging to different classes in the vehicle
b) The date of manufacture of the materials
c) The substance or material's hazard class
d) The quantity of material or substance on the shipment

18. While delivering compressed gas, the engine of your commercial vehicle runs a pump. When are you supposed to turn off your vehicle's engine once you're through with delivery?

a) Leave it on throughout
b) Unhook the hoses and then turn them off
c) First, turn it off and then unhook the hoses
d) Turn it off upon arrival and then utilize another power source to operate the pump

19. Which type of marking cannot be accepted for hazardous materials?

a) Identification number
b) Descriptive name using Roman print
c) UN marks
d) Name in Italics

20. To find out the number of hazardous materials that can be transported by a single vehicle, which hazard class employs the use of the transport index.

a) Class 4 (flammable solids)
b) Class 1 (explosives)
c) Class 3 (flammable liquids)
d) Class 7 (radioactive materials)

21. A technical name________________________________

–

a) Is a name often used in the streets to refer to a hazardous material
b) Is a microbiological or chemical name of hazardous material usually used in scientific texts and journals
c) Is a standard name commonly used within the trucking community to refer to hazardous material
d) Is a medical term used by medical personnel when referring to hazardous material

22. The HM column of your shipping paper entry has "RQ" or "X." What does that imply?

a) That the shipment is regulated by hazardous materials regulations
b) That the materials have to be top-loaded
c) That the materials contribute to the largest portion of the shipment
d) None of the above

23. Which of these hazard classes can NOT be put into a trailer that is temperature controlled (a trailer with an air conditioner/heater unit)?

a) Class 1, class 2.1, and class 3
b) Class 1, class 3, and class 4
c) Class 1, class 4, and class 5.1
d) None of the above

24. It is the responsibility of ____________to find out the special routes and permits required when hauling hazardous materials.

a) The inspector
b) The shipper
c) The carrier
d) The driver

25. A placarded vehicle transporting hazardous materials should have placards displayed on _____sides.

a) Three
b) Four
c) Two
d) One

26. If driving a placarded trailer with dual tires, how often are you required to check your tires?

a) Once after every three hours
b) When starting a trip and whenever you stop
c) Once after every 100 miles
d) Whenever you stop

27. What do shippers try to achieve when packaging the material?

a) To ensure the package can be identified easily
b) To ensure the package can be closed and opened easily
c) To make the package as light as possible
d) To achieve all of the above

28. Before fueling a placarded vehicle you must ensure ______________.

a) You check the air pressure
b) You've parked it near a fire extinguisher
c) You turn off the engine
d) You do all of the above

29. Which placards should be placed on a vehicle carrying 500 pounds of Divisions 1.1 and 1.2 explosives?

a) "Explosives" placards
b) "Dangerous" placards
c) "Blasting Agents" placards
d) All of the above

30. Who determines the hazardous materials identification number?

a) The receiver
b) The shipper
c) The driver
d) The carrier

Hazardous Materials (HAZMAT) Test – Answers

1. **Answer: a).** Explosives are supposed to be kept away from any material capable of emitting sparks. So, when transporting materials under Division 1.1 or 1.2, the floor liner should be made using non-ferrous or nonmetallic materials. Ferrous metals such as carbon steel and stainless steel should not be used whatsoever.

2. **Answer: c).** According to packaging regulations for hazardous materials, one of the key responsibilities of shippers is to make it easier for drivers, emergency personnel, and destination workers to easily and quickly identify what is contained in the package.

3. **Answer: b).** It costs a lot to clean up a spill, especially if it involves significant contamination. So, when you discover that your shipment is leaking, stop your truck as soon as possible and remove it from the road. Don't leave where you have packed the truck because of safety issues and liability and get someone to send for help. You need to make sure you give the person you're sending all the important information such as the direction of travel, where you've parked, hazard class, and the destination of your cargo. Put it all down in writing so that the person you're sending can deliver it.

4. **Answer: a).** Battery acid and silver cyanide belong to the category of materials that cannot be transported together due to safety concerns. The mixture of acids and silver cyanide can result in the release of an extremely dangerous gas called hydrocyanic acid. Therefore the best action you can take when faced with such as demand is to refuse to load the battery acid.

5. **Answer: b).** The two key locations where hazardous material identification numbers should be kept are on the packages and on the shipping papers since it is these places that emergency personnel usually check immediately.

6. **Answers: b).** You are required to place placards in a way that ensures that they can be read easily from whichever direction they face. You must keep them clean, unobscured by any object including tarpaulins, undamaged, and positioned 3 inches away from other markings.

7. **Answer: d).** Apart from the two key places where you are required to place the hazardous materials identification number, the number must also be displayed on all bulk packaging and cargo tanks.

8. **Answer: a).** The shipping papers must include information describing the hazardous materials and information concerning which action to take as well as whom to contact during an emergency.

9. **Answer: a).** The term "safe haven" is used to refer to a place set aside by local authorities where drivers can safely park their vehicles unattended, even if they carry explosive materials. This is a remedy for the trucking dilemma that has seen drivers take risks through improper decisions, like driving at night to ensure they are near their cargo.

10. **Answer d).** Placards refer to signs displayed on the outside of a vehicle to caution others that the load carried in the vehicle is hazardous material. The signs identify the cargo's hazard class.

11. **Answer: b).** When driving a placarded vehicle, it is a requirement that you have to stop between 15 and 50 feet away from the closest railroad crossing or bridge. Upon doing this, continue with your trip once you have ascertained that there is no train approaching, and avoid shifting while on the tracks.

12. **Answer c).** If a shipping paper contains descriptions for both non-hazardous and hazardous materials, the hazardous materials must be presented in a way that can be easily noted by the reader. The shipper is required to either highlight them using a contrasting color or ensure they are listed first.

13. **Answer: b).** It is a requirement for all placarded vehicles to have a fire extinguisher of UL rating 10 B:C at minimum. Meaning, it must be capable of putting out a 10-square-foot class B fire (consisting of nearly all flammable liquids) as well as electrically non-conductive (so, its C rating).

14. **Answer: d).** The key differences between portable and cargo tanks include their permanence. Whereas portable tanks are not

permanent, cargo tanks are. Because cargo tanks are permanently attached to vehicles, the filling has to be done on the vehicle and they are not required to showcase the name of the owner separately. Portable tanks can be filled on or off the commercial vehicle and then enjoined, and it has to showcase the name of the lessee or the owner.

15. **Answer: d).** The Emergency Response Guidebook (ERG) is a product of the US Department of Transportation, and among those who use it are emergency personnel like paramedics and firefighters to respond to emergencies involving trucks. In the guidebook, there is an index of hazardous materials identification numbers—a reason why it is necessary to label the shipping paperwork accurately.
16. **Answer: c).** If you are driving a placarded vehicle, you are required to stop between 15 and 50 feet away from the closest railroad crossing. Upon doing this, continue with your trip after you've ascertained that there is no train approaching, and avoid shifting on the tracks.
17. **Answer: b).** The information about the date of manufacture or when a product expires is not part of what you need to know unless it is provided as additional responsibility by your employer. However, you must be aware of the material you are transporting, its hazard class, as well as the overall quantity of all the hazardous materials or substances of all classes you'll be transporting with your commercial vehicle.
18. **Answer: c).** It is very risky to leave the engine of your vehicle on while pumping a load of compressed gas. Immediately after you finish delivering, you should turn off your engine, followed by unhooking any hoses.
19. **Answer: d).** A proper shipping name for hazardous materials has to strictly use Roman print (italics are not allowed). The markings consist of cautions, UN marks, ID number, weight, and instructions, or these can be combined in some way.
20. **Answer: d).** Each transport company relies on the transport index to determine the quantity of class 7 (radioactive materials) a truck driver can load. Radioactive materials produce radiation that can contaminate the other load. In the transport index of a package, you will find the specification on the maximum level of radiation (presented in ml/hr) expected per meter of a distance (around 39.37 inches).
21. **Answer: b).** The technical name refers to one utilized by scientists, and you can find it in technical handbooks, articles, and journals. It offers a standard terminology that can be used to refer to dangerous substances, rather than using slang terminologies that vary from one region to another.
22. **Answer: a).** If a shipping paper has information concerning hazardous or non-hazardous materials, then the hazardous materials need to be easily noticeable by a reader. This can be achieved in three ways: Put an "RQ" or "X" before the names. ("RQ" in full is reportable quantity). You can also do this by putt the hazardous materials first on the list or highlighting them using a contrasting color.
23. **Answer a).** There are three hazard classes that must not be placed in a trailer with automatic cooling and heating, these include explosives (1), flammable gases (2.1), and flammable liquids (3), due to their high level of volatility.
24. **Answer: d).** States or countries update their rules on the permits or create new restrictions on which routes to use. It is the work of the driver to ensure he/she is updated whenever there are any changes and collaborate with their carrier to acquire any permits that may be required.
25. **Answer: b).** Vehicles transporting hazardous materials should be placarded to caution people around about the risk. So, the placards must be displayed on all four sides of a vehicle (on the sides, front, and back).
26. **Answer: b).** if you are driving a placarded vehicle fitted with dual tires, it is a requirement that you check your tires before you start a trip and whenever you stop due to any reason be it to refuel or rest. To get the correct reading, use your tire pressure gauge.
27. **Answer: a).** Hazardous materials packaging regulations requires that the materials should be packaged in a manner that people such as drivers, emergency personnel, and destination personnel

can quickly and easily identify what is contained in the package.

28. **Answer: c).** You must turn off the engine before fueling your placarded vehicle, and someone must be in attendance when fueling it.

29. **Answer: a).** According to the Placard Table, certain materials must be placarded with particular information. On Placard Table 1, you will find explosives; therefore, on your vehicle, you must display placards showing "Explosives" and then division number (like 1.1, 1.2, or 1.3).

30. **Answer: b).** the packing of hazardous materials ready for transportation is done by the shipper. Therefore, the shipper has to find out the accurate identification number and write it on the packages as well as the shipping paper. (When an accident occurs, first responders usually start by looking for the identification number on the shipping papers and packages).

Combination Vehicle Test – Questions

1. During traffic crashes, about 40% of deaths that occur are a result of striking the instrument panel, windshield frame, or windshield. How can these deaths be prevented?

a) By wearing safety glasses
b) By wearing a lap belt
c) By wearing a shoulder belt
d) By wearing a windshield coating

2. What action are you supposed to take when you see an emergency vehicle approaching with flashing blue or red lights and sounding a siren?

a) Pull over and then stop
b) Increase your speed to give it way
c) Keep driving at the same speed
d) Slow down and continue moving

3. Two drivers have entered an uncontrolled intersection (an intersection without any control signals or signs) from different roadways almost at the same time. Which vehicle has the right-of-way?

a) The vehicle that signals first
b) The vehicle with more passengers
c) The vehicle on the right
d) The vehicle on the left

4. You should ____________ when you come across an elderly person crossing the road at an intersection.

a) Blow your horn
b) Keep driving
c) Stop and give the right of way
d) Increase your speed

5. What name is given to the danger zones in buses and trucks where the chances of crashing are high?

a) No-Zones
b) No-Passing zones
c) Empty-Zones
d) Round-Zones

6. Which of these vehicles has a higher likelihood of getting stuck at a railroad crossing that is raised?

a) Car carriers
b) Moving vans
c) Lowboys
d) All of the above

7. To which height must you ensure the landing gear is raised in order to drive?

a) Just slightly from the ground
b) All the way up
c) Exactly 6 feet from the ground
d) A portion of the way up

8. Which strategy should you employ to minimize the chances of rollover while driving a combination vehicle?

a) Ensure the cargo is kept as low as possible and slow down on the highway
b) Ensure the cargo is kept as low as possible and slow down around turns
c) Ensure the cargo is kept at a central point on the vehicle and slow down on the highway
d) Ensure the cargo is kept as high as possible and slow down around turns

9. To confirm whether air is flowing to all your trailers you can do all the following EXCEPT?

a) Press the pedal multiple times to reduce the air pressure
b) Push the red "trailer air supply" knob in
c) Go to the rear of your vehicle and open its emergency line shut-off valve
d) Open the emergency line shut-off valve

10. The shut-off valves are found at______________________.

a) The rear of a tractor
b) The rear of a trailer
c) The front of a trailer
d) The front of a tractor

11. The following are some statements referring to an antilock braking system (ABS). Which one is NOT true?

a) It enhances the braking ability of your vehicle
b) It is an additional system to the normal brakes
c) It activates whenever the wheels want to lock up
d) Each vehicle that has air brakes and was manufactured after March 1, 1998, onwards must have it

12. Why is it not advisable to utilize your trailer's hand valve when driving?

a) It produces noise that might be scary
b) It might cause your trailer to skid
c) It might increase the speed of your vehicle
d) All of the above

13. While uncoupling, you should ________________after unlocking the 5th wheel.

a) Lower the landing gear
b) Position the rig
c) Pull your tractor forward to clear it partially from the trailer
d) Disconnect your airlines

14. Which of the following must you do when you want to back a vehicle?

a) Walk around the vehicle and check carefully
b) Back up slowly
c) Utilize the mirrors on both sides
d) All of the above

15. When testing your tractor protection valve, you will do all the following EXCEPT?

a) Slowly pull forward, and then apply your trailer brakes
b) Charge the air brake system of your trailer.
c) Switch the engine off
d) Press the brake pedal multiple times in order to release air

16. Which of these has a higher likelihood of rolling over?

a) A triple's middle trailer
b) A double's rear trailer
c) A double's front trailer
d) A triple's rear trailer

17. When coupling your tractor-semitrailer, you should start by___________________.

a) Inspecting your fifth wheel
b) Checking the height of your trailer
c) Connecting all air lines to your trailer
d) Securing your tractor

18. Which of the following can be considered as "off-tracking"?

a) When an accident occurs and both the rear wheels and front wheels leave the roadway
b) When during a turn, the rear wheels take a different path from the front wheels
c) When the rear wheels leave the "track" or roadside
d) When you stop for a very long time on brakes and then you get "off the track" against what you had scheduled

19. The space between the upper and lower fifth wheel should be______ after coupling.

a) 24-36 inches
b) None
c) 5 feet
d) 1 foot

20. The following are roles performed by the emergency air line EXCEPT?

a) Controls the emergency brakes of a combination vehicle
b) Causes the emergency brakes of the trailer to apply in case the emergency air line runs out of pressure
c) Supplies air to relay valves that enhances the rate at which the foot brake operates
d) Supplies air to the air tanks of the trailer

Combination Vehicle Test – Answers

1. **Answer: c).** According to available statistics, striking the steering assembly accounts for 30% of deaths that occur in traffic crashes, while striking the instrument panel, windshield frame, and windshield accounts for 40%. However, you can reduce your chances of dying in a crash by wearing a shoulder and lap belt. The lap belt guards you against ejection and keeps your lower body protected. The shoulder belt protects your chest and head against striking the windshield or steering assembly.
2. **Answer: a).** If you see an emergency vehicle approaching with flashing blue or red lights and sounding a siren from whichever direction, you need to get clear of any nearby intersection, pull over to the roadside or the curb, and stop completely.
3. **Answer: c).** When two drivers enter an uncontrolled intersection (an intersection without any control signals or signs), from different roadways at almost the same time, the vehicle on the left is expected to give way for the vehicle on the right.
4. **Answer: c).** Whenever you are approaching an intersection and you see pedestrians crossing the road, you must stop your vehicle and let them cross before you proceed.
5. **Answer: a).** Hanging out around No-Zones is prohibited. No-Zones refer to large areas around buses, trucks, or other commercial vehicles in which a car may vanish into a blind spot or be too close to a point where the ability of the driver to maneuver or stop safely is restricted. No-Zones can be on the vehicle's sides, rear, or front.
6. **Answer: d).** One type of combination vehicle with a higher possibility of getting stuck at a raised railroad crossing is low-slung units such as moving vans, lowboys, and car carriers, among others. Exercise a lot of caution when driving this kind of vehicle at a railroad crossing.
7. **Answer: b).** The landing gear should be completely raised to ensure it does not get caught on railroad tracks or any other thing along the road as you drive.
8. **Answer: b).** Truck rollovers account for over 50% of fatalities among truck drivers. When the center of gravity of a truck is high, the possibility of a rollover is also high. Loading cargo on one side can cause the trailer to lean, increasing the likelihood of rollover. To minimize the possibility of rollover, the cargo should be kept as low as possible at the center, and the truck should slow down around turns.
9. **Answer: a).** You don't need to press the brake pedal multiple times to reduce the air pressure when checking airflow to all trailers. Rather, you should make sure the air pressure is at normal for you to push the red "trailer air supply" knob in. Then move to the back of the last trailer and open its emergency line shut-off valve. You should be able to hear air escaping to be certain that air is reaching all trailers.
10. **Answer: b).** You can find your vehicle's shut-off valves at the rear of your trailer because by being there they ensure the airlines are serviced. All the shut-off valves remain open except the ones in the last trailer.
11. **Answer: a).** Trailers that have air brakes and were manufactured after March 1, 1998, must be equipped with antilock brakes (ABS), the same as tractors fitted with air brakes manufactured after March 1, 1997. Antilock brakes should not influence your daily driving. It does not have any impact on the braking ability of your vehicle nor does it reduce the stopping distance. The primary purpose of ABS is to prevent the wheels from locking up to avoid a skid.
12. **Answer: b).** The trailer hand valve is only meant to apply your trailer brakes and not your tractor brakes. You should only apply the hand valve of your trailer when testing your brakes. It may cause your trailer to skid if you apply it while driving. If you intend to apply both trailer and tractor brakes, you can use the foot brake which has a lower likelihood of causing a jackknife or skid.
13. **Answer: c).** Once the fifth wheel has been unlocked, you should pull your tractor ensuring it is partially clear of your trailer. Lowering the

landing gear, positioning the rig, and disconnecting the air lines should happen before you unlock the fifth wheel. (Of course, you must start by positioning the rig).

14. **Answer: d).** When you want to back your vehicle, you must: start by walking around the vehicle to check your path. Then start backing along your path slowly. Ensure you check your mirrors regularly and correct any deviation from the trajectory immediately. As often as necessary, pull forward to reposition the vehicle.

15. **Answer: a).** When testing your tractor protection valve, you don't need to move your vehicle. Rather, you should charge the brake system of your trailer, turn your engine off, and then press your brake pedal severally to cut the air pressure. Once the air pressure has sufficiently reduced, your trailer's air supply control (commonly referred to as the tractor protection valve control) will pop out.

16. **Answer: d).** The chances of a trailer rolling over are higher than a tractor. Additionally, in a triple or double combination, the likelihood of each trailer rolling over is higher compared to the one in front of it. A triple's rear trailer is 3.5 times more likely to roll over compared to the tractor alone. This is referred to as the "crack-the-whip effect" or rearward amplification.

17. **Answer: a)**. When coupling your tractor-semitrailer, you will do everything listed options. But first, you will have to check your fifth wheel. Thereafter, you can ensure the tractor is secure, inspect the height of your trailer, and then make sure all the air lines are connected.

18. **Answer: b).** Off-tracking refers to a situation where during a turn your rear and front wheels take different paths. Longer vehicles often experience more off-tracking compared to shorter ones. Consequently, a tractor's path tends to be wider compared to the path followed by the rig itself.

19. **Answer: b).** There should be no space between the upper and lower fifth wheel. If that happens, then something needs fixing. Do not drive until you identify and fix the issue.

20. **Answer: c).** It is not the role of the air line to supply relay valves with air to enhance the rate at which foot and hand brakes operate. Rather, this function is carried out by the service line.

Tanker Vehicles Test – Questions

1. What is a baffled tanker?

a) It's one with separate tanks in the trailer
b) It's one with bulkheads and holes that allow liquid to flow through
c) It's one with hollow balls that float in the liquid to slow movement

2. Which kind of surge still occurs even in baffled tanks?

a) Front-to-back
b) Top-to-bottom
c) Side-to-side

3. What is the impact of a liquid surge on a tanker?

a) The Surge increases the truck's wind drag.
b) The surge makes turning around corners tighter
c) The surge can push your truck in the direction of the liquid waves

4. When can you use your truck escape ramp?

a) You should never use it
b) Whenever you experience brake problems
c) Only when it's a baffled tanker

5. When loading or unloading a liquid tanker, how far back should a helper stand?

a) 25 feet
b) 20 feet
c) 15 feet

6. Un-baffled liquid tanks are also called ______________.

a) Aluminum tanks
b) Smooth-bore tanks
c) Non-baffled liquid tanks

7. ___________is the movement of liquids in tanks that are partially filled.

a) Surging
b) Waves
c) Splashing

8. Which vehicles require a tank endorsement?

a) Vehicles that transport gases or liquids
b) Vehicles that transport passengers
c) Vehicles that transport hazardous materials

9. The following statements refer to tankers and the center of gravity. Which one is TRUE?

a) At the posted speed limits, tankers have a higher likelihood of turning over on curves
b) Most of the weight of the load is carried up off the ground
c) They are more likely to overturn than other vehicles, even within the speed limit

10. While driving your tanker, you encounter an emergency that requires you to stop quickly. What must you do to avoid crashing?

a) Apply the emergency brakes
b) Apply hard brakes until the wheels are locked
c) Apply stab or controlled braking

11. When should you be more careful while driving smooth-bore tankers?

a) When driving against the wind
b) When driving downhill or uphill
c) While stopping or starting

12. Why is it important to be aware of the outage required for the liquids you transport?

a) The expansion rate of some liquids when they get warm is higher than that of others
b) Some liquids contract at a higher rate when temperatures are low
c) Some heavy liquids don't require any outage

13. You need to have special skills when hauling liquids in tanks because of______________.

a) The higher center of gravity
b) The liquid movement
c) All of the above

14. What is likely to occur as a result of the side-to-side surge?

a) Failure of the suspension system
b) Over-speeding
c) Rollover

15. What should you check when loading a cargo tank's small tanks that have bulkheads?

a) The ratio of air to fuel
b) Weight distribution
c) Water content

16. You should inspect your tank vehicle____________________.

a) Before starting your trip
b) Before loading it
c) Before loading, starting your trip, or unloading it

17. Which of the following is among the factors that determine the amount of liquid you can haul?

a) The liquid's weight
b) The liquid's expansion rate
c) All of the above factors

18. When conducting a tank inspection, you should check__________________.

a) Tank's shell or body, vents, and manhole covers
b) Hoses, connections, and pipes
c) All of the above

19. What is an outage?

a) The allowance for liquid expansion
b) Weight of a liquid
c) The rate at which liquid tanks drain

20. Separators that are used in dividing spaces into liquid-tight compartments are known as___________.

a) Baffles
b) Barriers
c) Bulkheads

Tanker Vehicles Test – Answers

1. **Answer: b).** A baffled liquid tank is a tank that has bulkheads with holes to allow liquid to flow through with less force as compared to a tank without such bulkheads.
2. **Answer: c).** The bulkheads in baffled tanks mainly reduce forward-and-backward surge and not side-to-side surge.
3. **Answer: c).** The liquid surge can sway the vehicle in the direction of the liquid waves. This is especially risky on an icy road where the likelihood of a truck being pushed forward is higher, and it might even be pushed past a red light and enters an intersection.
4. **Answer: b).** An escape ramp is made of upgrades, soft gravel, or both, which slows down your vehicle whenever you experience brake fail while driving downhill. Irrespective of the type of commercial vehicle you are operating, when you experience difficulties in slowing down your downhill speed, you can go for any of the escape ramps to save your life, cargo, or equipment.
5. **Answer: a).** The person monitoring the pumping or unloading of a liquid tanker should be in a position where he/she can clearly see the cargo tank, be alert, and be within 25 feet from the tank. The person should also be aware of the hazards of the material and know what to do during an emergency.
6. **Answer: b).** Another name for an un-baffled tank is a "smooth bore" tank. Un-baffled tanks are used to transport liquids such as milk and other liquid food items since maintaining their cleanness is easier than baffled tanks.
7. **Answer: a).** Liquids have a tendency to move around in tanks that are not completely filled. The liquid can move from side to side or backward and forward. This movement is called "surging."
8. **Answer: a).** Federal regulations require that if you want to operate a tank vehicle that requires you to possess a CDL, you must also have a tank endorsement. The definition "tank vehicle" refers to any vehicle used to transport more than 119 gallons of gas or liquid in a single tank or 1.000 gallons or more in multiple tanks, that are attached either temporarily or permanently to the vehicle.
9. **Answer: c).** The center of gravity for tank vehicles is usually higher, about five to six feet off the road. As a result, tankers are top-heavy, which increases their chances of rollovers compared to other kinds of vehicles. Tests have also proved that even at posted curve speed limits tank vehicles are more likely to roll over. To safely manage a curve, make sure you slow down below the posted speed.
10. **Answer: c).** Hard or sudden brakes might cause a forward surge in the liquid in your tank, which might force the vehicle to move forward. In case you face a situation that forces you to stop quickly, utilize your stab or controlled brakes. (However, if the vehicle has antilock brakes, avoid using stab braking).
11. **Answer: c).** Smooth-bore or unbaffled tanks do not have baffles that eliminate forward-and-backward surge. Whenever you want to start your tanker from a stopped position, the liquid will experience a backward surge, which will push the vehicle backward. When you attempt stopping, the liquid will surge forward, and the vehicle will be further pushed forward. Be very careful while performing such actions.
12. **Answer: a).** The expansion rate of liquids with the temperature rise varies from one liquid to another. It is always important to know the amount of outage required for the liquid type you'll be transporting.
13. **Answer: c).** Operating a tanker loaded with liquid cargo requires special skills because of the higher center of gravity of the vehicle as well as the higher chances that the liquid may surge backward or forward or from one side to another. When the center of gravity is higher, the likelihood of rolling over also increases. On the other hand, the liquid surge is likely to dangerously push your vehicle sideways or forward, another possible cause of a rollover.
14. **Answer: c).** When liquid surges from side-to-side, lateral (sideways) forces are exerted on the tank.

The moment a side-to-side surge starts, if the driver does not act fast, the tank will continue swaying increasing the chances of a rollover.

15. **Answer: b).** whenever loading or unloading smaller tanks that are divided by bulkheads, you should be very keen on weight distribution. Do not put a lot of weight on the back or front of the vehicle.

16. **Answer: c).** You must inspect your tank vehicle before loading, starting your trip, and unloading it. The inspection helps you ascertain that your vehicle can hold its gas or liquid contents safely.

17. **Answer: c).** Dense liquids (for instance some acids) are usually very heavy and if you fill the tank, they might surpass acceptable legal weights. Therefore, if hauling heavy liquids you just need to partially fill your tank. The rate of expansion of a liquid while in transit also determines what amount of liquid you will load into your tank. Knowing the expansion rate will enable you to know how much outage to leave.

18. **Answer: c).** when doing your tank inspection, ensure you check your tank's shell or body for leaks or dents. Check hoses, connections, and pipes for leaks, more so on joints. Check vents as well as manhole covers, ensuring the covers close properly and that they have covers. Ensure the vents are clear for proper functioning. Don't forget to check the cut-off valves, discharge, and intake.

19. **Answer: a).** When the temperatures are high, liquids expand, and outage refers to the allowance that is left in a tank to cater to the expansion. The expansion rate of liquids differs. So, the amount of outage required depends on the kind of liquid.

20. **Answer: c).** Bulkheads are separators used to divide spaces into liquid-tight compartments. Tanker vehicles often have bulkheads in their tanks to divide them into separate compartments.

School Bus Test – Questions

1. **Which of the following statements correctly describes a passive railroad crossing?**

a) It is a railroad crossing without any form of traffic control device
b) It is a railroad crossing where the driver is not required to stop
c) It is a railroad crossing without a crossbuck sign

2. **Depending on the width and length of your school bus, the blind spot behind it may extend up to______________ feet.**

a) 100
b) 400
c) 200

3. **What is the key role of the overhead interior rear-view mirror in a school bus?**

a) It monitors the blind spot that is immediately behind your bus
b) It monitors the activities of passengers inside the bus
c) It monitors the approaching traffic

4. **Why do the outside right and left side flat mirrors require adjustment?**

a) To enable you to see 200 feet behind your bus
b) To enable you to see your right and left rear tires meeting the road
c) All of the above reasons

5. **What is the first thing you need to do immediately after stopping your school bus?**

a) Activate your alternately flashing red lights as well as make sure you extend the stop arm
b) Ensure the students are loaded as fast as possible
c) Activate your alternately flashing yellow lights

6. **You are loading students on the bus, and you've realized a student is missing. What action should you take?**

a) Ensure the bus is secured, remove the key, and then check underneath and around your bus for the missing student
b) Inquire from the students whether they saw the missing student
c) Look in the mirrors for the missing student

7. **Among the school officials, the only official that is ever met by up to_____ % of parents is the school driver.**

a) 65
b) 85
c) 50

8. **Apart from a functioning fire extinguisher, three red reflective triangles, and spare electrical fuses (for equipped vehicles), what else should be included in a school bus as safety gear?**

a) Alcohol and a first-aid kit
b) A body fluid cleanup kit and first-aid kit
c) A bolt cutter and three flares

9. **Which statement is TRUE concerning evacuation procedures?**

a) If there is time, let the dispatch office know about the situation, the location, as well as what kind of help you need
b) If there is time, close all the bus windows
c) Before evacuation, if time allows you, back up to a safe place

10. **What is the right thing to do when unloading students at school?**

a) Ask the students to keep seated until they get a signal to alight
b) Leave your engine on so you can immediately drive away once you have unloaded all the students
c) Stand outside your bus and monitor the students as they exit

11. School buses are painted_____________.

a) National School Bus Glossy Yellow
b) Amber
c) Fluorescent yellow

12. What are you supposed to check on your school bus during the post-trip inspection?

a) The litter on the floor
b) The cleanness of the seats
c) Operational or mechanical problems

13. In the majority of states, school bus drivers are required to take physical exams after every_______

a) 5 years
b) 1 year
c) 3 years

14. Which statement is TRUE about antilock brakes in your vehicle?

a) It ensures your wheels do not lock when you apply hard brakes
b) It only functions when the ABS switch is activated on your instrument panel
c) It shortens the stopping distance of your vehicle

15. If you encounter a malfunctioning railroad crossing signal, which action should you take?

a) Look for an alternative route
b) Contact your dispatch officer for instructions
c) Proceed, but be extremely cautious

16. Before unloading students from the school bus, you should instruct them that once they exit they should_______________.

a) Walk 10 to 15 feet away from the school bus's side
b) Cross in front of the bus
c) Walk behind the bus

17. The most dangerous moment during a bus ride is______________.

a) When crossing an intersection
b) When unloading and loading students
c) When approaching a railroad crossing

18. Which one of the following is TRUE about the special dangers associated with the loading and unloading of students?

a) Instruct students that they are free to pick up any dropped items provided they are not underneath the bus
b) Instruct students not to pick any dropped items, leave the danger zones, and attract your attention to get the items
c) Instruct students to avoid using the handrails as they exit the bus since they may be caught

19. If you encounter an unruly student on the bus who is threatening other students' safety, the best action to take is to____________________.

a) Pull your bus to the roadside and explain the rules and regulations firmly to the unruly student
b) Immediately get the unruly student out of the bus
c) Give the unruly student a seat next to you

20. The only time you can change your school bus stop location is _____________.

a) Only if the majority of the passengers allow you to change
b) Only if you have written approval from your school district
c) Only if there is a nearby location that seems better

School Bus Test – Answers

1. **Answer: a).** A passive railroad crossing refers to a railroad crossing that does not have any form of traffic control equipment (for example, gates, bells, or lights) to caution a driver about an approaching train. When approaching the crossing, the driver has to stop, and check if there is any train approaching, before crossing.
2. **Answer: b).** Normally, the blind spot behind a school bus goes up to between 50 and 150 feet behind the bus. However, depending on the bus's width and length, this can still extend up to 400 feet.
3. **Answer: b).** The primary function of the overhead inside rear-view mirror in a school bus is to check the activities of passengers on the bus.
4. **Answer: c).** You should adjust the left and right flat side mirrors to enable you to have a view of around 200 feet behind the bus and also see the rear tires touch the ground.
5. **Answer: a).** Immediately after stopping your bus, and before you load or unload it, ensure you set the transmission in park (if you don't have park shift point, set it to neutral), switch on your alternately shifting red lights, as well as ensuring you extend your stop arm.
6. **Answer: a).** When you're almost stopping, do a head count of the students before they come out of the bus, and repeat the same as they load into your bus. In case there is a student you cannot account for, secure your bus to ensure it doesn't move, carry along your ignition key, and check both around as well as underneath your bus.
7. **Answer: b).** The majority of parents only get an opportunity to meet the school driver, among the school representatives. Therefore, handle them with a lot of courtesy and listen to their concerns.
8. **Answer: b).** Aside from the usual emergency equipment required in a CMV, a school bus needs to have a body fluid clean-up kit and a first-aid kit.
9. **Answer: a).** You might have to make a quick decision on whether there is a need to evacuate your bus. The ideal thing to do is to first contact your dispatch official to explain your situation and ask for help; however, do this only if there is time.
10. **Answer: a).** When students are exiting the bus at school, make sure the bus is secured, ask the students to remain on their seats until they get a signal to exit, and be in a position where you can supervise them as they come down. Once you've done, you can give the students a signal to start coming out of the bus as you keep an eye on them. Make sure you count the students one by one as they exit.
11. **Answer: a).** According to the National Highway Transportation Safety Administration (NHTSA) guidelines, all school buses must be National School Bus Glossy Yellow in color. Following this guideline, all states have adopted this as a mandatory requirement for all school buses. The color was initially picked because it is easily visible.
12. **Answer: c).** Immediately after checking for stray students, you are required to do a post-trip inspection on your bus. During this check, you need to focus on the operational and mechanical systems of the bus for any issues. Once you encounter any problem, report it immediately to the school authorities or your supervisor.
13. **Answer: b).** In many states, school bus drivers are required to take a physical examination after every 1 year to ascertain that they are still qualified to operate a school bus. The examination includes a vision test.
14. **Answer: a).** ABS makes sure your wheels do not lock, enabling you to brake harder even on slippery roads. ABS doesn't have a significant impact on other aspects of your driving. Your braking efficiency is not affected by it neither does it reduce the stopping distance.
15. **Answer: b).** In case there are no police around, and you are certain the railroad crossing signal is not functioning as it should, contact your dispatcher and inform them about the situation. Find out from them how you should proceed.

16. **Answer: a).** Before you unload your school bus at a bus stop, it is important to instruct the students how far from the bus they should walk (usually about 10 feet away from the bus's side) to a position where you can see all the students plainly.
17. **Answer: b).** During the loading and unloading of students, the chances of the students getting injured increase three times.
18. **Answer: b).** To ensure student safety during loading and unloading, students must remain within the driver's view. Trying to retrieve a dropped item might make a student disappear from the driver's view and get into the danger zone. Students should be instructed to get off the danger zones and notify the driver whenever they have dropped their items.
19. **Answer: a).** One way of dealing with serious issues while driving is to stop your bus in a safe location away from the road—maybe a driveway or a parking lot, remove the ignition key and carry it if you have to leave your seat, and then stand up and address the student. Use courteous language but a firm voice. Stress the expected behavior to the student without showing anger, but demonstrate that you are serious about it.
20. **Answer: b).** Changing a bus stop location is never permitted except with written approval by an appropriate official from your school district.

Passenger Vehicle Test – Questions

1. When you are driving on a banked curve and your bus starts leaning toward the outside, it implies that__________________.

a) The road is wet
b) One of your tires is flat
c) Your speed is too low
d) Your speed is very high

2. Which action should you take when you encounter a disruptive or drunk passenger?

a) Drive up to a safe, adequately–lit location that is not lonely and drop the person off
b) Drop off the person at your next scheduled stop
c) Refer to what your carrier's guidelines say about handling stubborn passengers
d) Take any of the above actions

3. Which of these statements is NOT true concerning the interior of a bus?

a) Any available emergency door light must be functional
b) The bus should never be driven while the window or exit door is open
c) When the headlights are switched on, the red emergency door light can remain off
d) The seats have to be fastened securely to the bus and they should be secure for riders

4. Are passenger buses permitted to transport classes 1, 3, 4, and 5 of hazardous materials each weighing 100 pounds at the same time?

a) No
b) Yes; however for short distances only
c) Yes; however, only during the night
d) Yes

5. You must check all the following before you start driving EXCEPT?

a) The steering mechanism
b) The parking brake
c) The windshield wipers
d) The FM/AM radio

6. You must ensure that ______________is closed when driving your bus.

a) The emergency window
b) All the windows
c) The roof hatches
d) The driver's window

7. The following are statements regarding hazardous materials. Which one is NOT true?

a) A bus cannot transport a large quantity of hazardous materials
b) Shippers are required to mark each hazardous material's package with the hazard label, ID number, and name of the material
c) A bus can transport any hazardous materials provided they are labeled properly
d) Small arms with the "ORM-D" label can be transported by bus

8. When doing a vehicle inspection on your transit bus or coach, you must check the baggage compartments and ensure that its doors can_______ securely.

a) Open
b) Lift
c) Close
d) Latch

9. The driver is expected to announce____________ at each stop or whenever the bus reaches a destination.

a) The location
b) The bus number
c) The next departure time of the bus
d) All of the above

10. Where do most of the bus accidents happen?

a) At intersections
b) On roundabouts
c) In parking lots
d) On highways

11. When conducting your pre-trip inspection, you are only expected to append your signature on the previous driver's inspection report if_______________.

a) The faults recorded on it are certified as repaired or have no need for repair
b) No faults are recorded on it
c) You personally have witnessed each of the recorded defects being fixed
d) You have a personal relationship with the other driver and you trust her or him

12. To operate a bus with a seating capacity of _________ or more occupants, you included, you must have a CDL with (P) endorsement.

a) 32
b) 16
c) 21
d) 24

13. If you're driving a bus with a manual transmission, you _______ while driving across railroad tracks.

a) Should upshift
b) Should not shift gears
c) Should coast in neutral
d) Should downshift

14. The right time to complete a driver's inspection report is_____________.

a) Before you start your trip
b) Only when there is a suspected issue
c) When you are required to submit it
d) When you complete your shift

15. Which of the following statements is TRUE about buses having re-grooved or recapped tires?

a) Buses can only have them on the front wheels
b) Buses can only have them outside of duals
c) Buses can only have them on all wheels or any of the wheels
d) Buses can have them anywhere but not on the front wheels

16. The only time you can drive your bus with an opened emergency exit door is_______________.

a) When not driving for a longer distance
b) If the temperature level in the cabin is excessively hot
c) If the people on board want it to be open
d) There is no particular time you are permitted to drive your bus with an open emergency exit door

17. What details must be captured in your post-trip inspection report if you are an employee of an interstate carrier?

a) Any faults that might lead to breakdown or compromise safety
b) Total mileage, distance covered, and fuel consumption
c) The number of buses you have operated
d) Any issues that happened with the riders

18. In reference to hazardous materials, what does ORM-D stand for?

a) Other Regulated Materials – Domestic
b) Other Reasonable Materials – Dangerous
c) Other Regulatory Materials – Domestic
d) Other Requisition Materials – Dangerous

19. The following emergency gear should NEVER miss on your bus:

a) Fire extinguisher, spare electric fuses, first aid kit
b) Reflectors, spare electric fuses, fire extinguisher
c) Tire repair kit, fire extinguisher, reflectors
d) All of the above

20. To be safe while driving a bus of 40 feet at a speed of 50 mph on a dry road with good visibility, how much distance in front of the bus should you keep?

a) 10 seconds
b) 8 seconds
c) 6 seconds
d) 5 seconds

Passenger Vehicle Test – Answers

1. **Answer: d).** When driving on a banked curve and then your bus starts to lean towards the outside, it means your speed is too high and you need to slow down to avoid rolling over or skidding. Only cars are safe with the posted speed limit, not buses.
2. **Answer: d).** In case you have a disruptive or drunk passenger on your bus, there are a few actions you are allowed to take to maintain the safety of the rest of the passengers. Where applicable, you can refer to what your carrier's guidelines say concerning handling that kind of passenger. Better still, you can drop off the passenger at your next scheduled stop as well as any place with adequate light and people.
3. **Answer: c).** If there is a red emergency exit light at the bus's emergency door, it has to work. Nonetheless, you are only required to switch it on when experiencing poor visibility such that you have to turn on the headlights (For example it could be when experiencing bad weather or at night).
4. **Answer: d).** Buses are only allowed to carry a maximum of 100 pounds of each hazardous material permitted (i.e., classes 1, 3, 4, and 5) at the same time and the total weight of all permitted hazardous materials in the bus should not exceed 500 pounds (In the above case, the total weight will be 400 pounds, which is acceptable). Transporting of Division 2.3 (poison gas) as well as liquid class 6 (poison) is however completely prohibited. Radioactive materials and explosives are totally unacceptable in the passenger area.
5. **Answer: d).** Checking all the sensitive systems such as emergency equipment, tires, brakes, and steering, before you start driving is important. To ensure passenger safety is guaranteed, you also need to inspect the emergency exits, signaling devices, railings, handholds, and seats. Having DVD music or FM on your bus is great; however, even without them, you can still take your passengers to their destination safely.
6. **Answer: a).** Anytime you are driving your bus the emergency exit doors and windows must be shut.
7. **Answer: c).** The majority of hazardous materials cannot be carried on buses. But particular hazardous materials (such as "ORM-D" labeled small-arms ammunition) are permitted on a bus provided their packaging is labeled properly. You should never carry any hazardous materials before you confirm what the rules say about them.
8. **Answer: d).** When inspecting your transit bus or coach, one of the things you need to make sure you check is whether the door of the baggage compartment can latch securely. You should also inspect whether the compartment doors are operating properly and if they have any faults that need fixing.
9. **Answer: d).** whenever a bus arrives at a destination or any intermediate stop, the driver should announce the bus number, the next departure time of the bus, why the bus is stopping, and the location.
10. **Answer: a).** because of the presence of many pedestrians involved in various activities and drivers, road intersections experience a lot of bus accidents. Even though there are signals and signs that are meant to control traffic at intersections, make sure you exercise a lot of caution.
11. **Answer: a).** It is only advisable to append your signature on a previous driver's report if the faults recorded on it have been confirmed to be fixed or no need for repair. Of course, you will do your own pre-trip inspection.
12. **Answer: b).** For you to operate a bus with a seating capacity of 16 or more individuals, you included, you need a CDL with a passenger (P) endorsement.
13. **Answer: b).** when driving a manual transmission bus across a high railroad crossing, don't shift gears. If you shift gears on a high railroad crossing, your bus is highly likely to get stuck or stall on the rail tracks.
14. **Answer: d).** Drivers serving an interstate carrier are required to prepare a post-trip inspection report for every vehicle they operate during a shift. List every safety-related issues that you

encountered during your shift and repairs that you think are necessary. The next driver will rely on the inspection report to address any safety issues before starting his/her shift. According to Federal regulations, an inspection report should be prepared at the end of your driving day.

15. **Answer: d).** You can have retreated, recapped, or re-grooved tires on any of your bus's wheels but not on your front wheels, it is completely prohibited.

16. **Answer: d).** Your bus's emergency exit door should always remain shut. No situation permits you to drive while it's open.

17. **Answer: a).** Whenever you complete a shift, inspect your bus. If you are employed by an interstate carrier, it is always mandatory to prepare a written report for any bus you drove. In the report, you must specify every bus and record any faults that are likely to cause a breakdown or affect safety. Even if the bus doesn't have any problems, you should indicate that on the report.

18. **Answer: a).** ORM-D stands for Other Regulated Materials – Domestic.

19. **Answer: b).** The law requires you to always have in your bus emergency reflectors, fire extinguisher, and spare electrical fuses except if your bus is fitted with circuit breakers.

20. **Answer: d).** To find out your vehicle's following distance, add one second for every 10 feet of the length of the vehicle for speeds that are below 40 mph. If the speed exceeds 40 mph, apply the same formula but add one second for the extra speed.

Dear Future Commercial Driver,

first of all, thank you again for purchasing our product.

Secondly, congratulations! If you are using our Guide, you are among those few who are willing to do whatever it takes to excel on the exam and are not satisfied with just trying.
We create our Study Guides in the same spirit. We want to offer our students only the best to help them get only the best through precise, accurate, and easy-to-use information.

That is why **your success is our success**, and if you think our Guide helped you achieve your goals, we would love it if you could take 60 seconds of your time to leave us a review on Amazon.

Thank you again for trusting us by choosing our Guide, and good luck with your new life as a commercial driver.

Sincerely,

H.S.P. Test Team

Scan the QR code to leave a review (it only takes you 60 seconds):

References

ADOT Motor Vehicle Division. (2015). Arizona Commercial Driver License Manual. ADOT Motor Vehicle Division. https://driving-tests.org/wp-content/uploads/2016/08/AZ_40-7802_15.pdf

American Association of Motor Vehicle Administrators. (2021). Commercial Drivers License Manual (2021st–2023rd ed.). https://driving-tests.org/wp-content/uploads/2021/10/ND_CDL-manual.pdf

Andrade, F. (2019). fernando-andrade-ZimIwyvYeBM-unsplash. In upsplash.com.

campbell. (2018). justin-campbell-FacLsqkeX4w-unsplash. In unsplash.com.

Department of Motor Vehicles. (2020). California Commercial Driver Handbook (2019th–2021st ed.). https://driving-tests.org/wp-content/uploads/2020/03/comlhdbk.pdf

Driving TV. (2020a, June 20). 2020 CDL QUESTIONS GENERAL KNOWLEDGE EXAM #1/CDL PERMIT PRACTICE TEST. Www.youtube.com. https://www.youtube.com/watch?v=sKXH_rS10b8&list=PLE3pr09P2AS9oKCWLlwQPPafVihuIuXCX&index=1&t=12s

Driving TV. (2020b, December 13). 2021 CDL GENERAL KNOWLEDGE PRACTICE TEST PART 1 (Questions & Answers). Www.youtube.com. https://www.youtube.com/watch?v=OIXPZ-tPwYQ&list=PLzo8Xp5O7px1zKXVAQxf34-87xtCUZrV9&index=18

Driving TV. (2021a, January 1). 2021 CDL GENERAL KNOWLEDGE PRACTICE TEST PART 2 (Questions & Answers). Www.youtube.com. https://www.youtube.com/watch?v=5D9blnCADzI&list=PLzo8Xp5O7px1zKXVAQxf34-87xtCUZrV9&index=21

Driving TV. (2021b, January 23). 2021 CDL GENERAL KNOWLEDGE PRACTICE TEST PART 3 (Questions & Answers). Www.youtube.com. https://www.youtube.com/watch?v=BnNLifST6Lo&list=PLzo8Xp5O7px1zKXVAQxf34-87xtCUZrV9&index=23

Driving TV. (2021c, April 27). 2021 CDL GENERAL KNOWLEDGE PRACTICE TEST PART 4 (Questions & Answers). Www.youtube.com. https://www.youtube.com/watch?v=5uyEPR3EXD4&list=PLzo8Xp5O7px1zKXVAQxf34-87xtCUZrV9&index=24

Driving-tests.org. (n.d.). FREE Minnesota CDL Combination Practice Test 2021. Driving-Tests.org. Retrieved November 14, 2021, from https://driving-tests.org/minnesota/mn-cdl-combination-test/

Federal Motor Carrier Safety Administration. (n.d.). Training_Provider_Registration. Tpr.fmcsa.dot.gov. Retrieved November 14, 2021, from https://tpr.fmcsa.dot.gov/content/Resources/Training_Provider_Registration/story.html

Gasperini, F. (2017). flavio-gasperini-YBzsJv3c1EQ-unsplash. In Upsplash.com.

Henry, M. (2017). parked-schoolbus-in-the-fog. In burst.shopify.com.

JESHOOTS.com. (2018). jeshoots-com--2vD8lIhdnw-unsplash. In upsplash.com.

Lesics. (2017, December 31). Clutch, How does it work ?

Www.youtube.com.https://www.youtube.com/watch?v=devo3kdSPQY&list=PLE3pr09P2AS9oKCWLlwQPPafVihuIuXCX&index=8

Limcaco, J. (2017). jad-limcaco-Y_J0phaFy2g-unsplash. In upsplash.com.

Mitrione, J. (2020). jason-mitrione-PNb6Zn-f5R4-unsplash. In unsplash.com.

Moult, R. (2017). rhys-moult-7eaFIKeo1MQ-unsplash. In unsplash.com.

Omni. (n.d.). Stopping Distance Calculator. Www.omnicalculator.com. Retrieved November 14, 2021, from https://www.omnicalculator.com/physics/stopping-distance

PrePass. (2020). What You Need to Know About New Entry-Level Driver Training Rules for Truckers (1.7 ed.). http://www.prepassalliance.org/wp-content/uploads/2020/05/PP_WhitePaper_DriverTraining_20200204.pdf

Publio, F. (2017). city-trucks-tackle-blizzard. In burst.shopify.com.

Reltman, I. (Director). (1984, June 8). Ghostbusters [Film]. Columbia Pictures.

Tafra, S. (2021). stephen-tafra-n6FQT4g1Y8Q-unsplash. In Upsplash.com.

Credits

Cover:

1.

this cover has been designed using assets from Freepik.com.

Item 1 URL (background): https://www.freepik.com/premium-photo/road-surface-sky-natural-landscape_[illegible].htm

object downloaded with premium license

2.

This cover has been designed using assets from Unspalsh.com.

Item 2 URL (truck): https://unsplash.com/it/foto/[illegible]

Pic by: Jeremy Bishop

Use for commercial purposes allowed

Made in the USA
Columbia, SC
01 September 2024

41406743R00074